TOTTENHAM HOTSPUR

Champions of England
1950-51 & 1960-61

DESERT ISLAND FOOTBALL HISTORIES

Club Histories

	ISBN
Aberdeen: A Centenary History 1903-2003	1-874287-57-0
Aberdeen: Champions of Scotland 1954-55	1-874287-65-1
Aberdeen: The European Era – A Complete Record	1-874287-11-2
Bristol City: The Modern Era – A Complete Record	1-874287-28-7
Bristol City: The Early Years 1894-1915	1-874287-74-0
Cambridge United: The League Era – A Complete Record	1-874287-32-5
Cambridge United: 101 Golden Greats	1-874287-58-9
The Story of the Celtic 1888-1938	1-874287-15-5
Chelsea: Champions of England 1954-55	1-874287-77-5
Colchester United: Graham to Whitton – A Complete Record	1-874287-27-9
Coventry City: The Elite Era – A Complete Record	1-874287-83-X
Coventry City: An Illustrated History	1-874287-59-7
Dundee: Champions of Scotland 1961-62	1-874287-86-4
Dundee United: Champions of Scotland 1982-83	1-874287-71-6
History of the Everton Football Club 1878-1928	1-874287-14-7
Halifax Town: From Ball to Lillis – A Complete Record	1-874287-26-0
Hereford United: The League Era – A Complete Record	1-874287-18-X
Hereford United: The Wilderness Years 1997-2004	1-874287-83-X
Huddersfield Town: Champions of England 1923-1926	1-874287-88-0
Ipswich Town: The Modern Era – A Complete Record	1-874287-43-0
Ipswich Town: Champions of England 1961-62	1-874287-63-5
Kilmarnock: Champions of Scotland 1964-65	1-874287-87-2
Luton Town: The Modern Era – A Complete Record	1-874287-90-2
Luton Town: An Illustrated History	1-874287-79-1
Manchester United's Golden Age 1903-1914: Dick Duckworth	1-874287-80-5
The Matt Busby Chronicles: Manchester United 1946-69	1-874287-53-8
Motherwell: Champions of Scotland 1931-32	1-874287-73-2
Norwich City: The Modern Era – A Complete Record	1-874287-67-8
Peterborough United: The Modern Era – A Complete Record	1-874287-33-3
Peterborough United: Who's Who?	1-874287-48-1
Plymouth Argyle: The Modern Era – A Complete Record	1-874287-54-6
Plymouth Argyle: 101 Golden Greats	1-874287-64-3
Plymouth Argyle: Snakes & Ladders – Promotions and Relegations	1-874287-82-1
Portsmouth: From Tindall to Ball – A Complete Record	1-874287-25-2
Portsmouth: Champions of England – 1948-49 & 1949-50	1-874287-50-3
The Story of the Rangers 1873-1923	1-874287-16-3
The Romance of the Wednesday 1867-1926	1-874287-17-1
Stoke City: The Modern Era – A Complete Record	1-874287-76-7
Stoke City: 101 Golden Greats	1-874287-55-4
Potters at War: Stoke City 1939-47	1-874287-78-3
Tottenham Hotspur: Champions of England 1950-51, 1960-61	1-874287-84-8
West Ham: From Greenwood to Redknapp	1-874287-19-8
West Ham: The Elite Era – A Complete Record	1-874287-31-7
Wimbledon: From Southern League to Premiership	1-874287-09-0
Wimbledon: From Wembley to Selhurst	1-874287-20-1
Wimbledon: The Premiership Years	1-874287-40-6
Wrexham: The European Era – A Complete Record	1-874287-52-X

World Cup Histories

England's Quest for the World Cup – A Complete Record	1-874287-61-9
Scotland: The Quest for the World Cup – A Complete Record	1-897850-50-6
Ireland: The Quest for the World Cup – A Complete Record	1-897850-80-8

Miscellaneous

Red Dragons in Europe – A Complete Record	1-874287-01-5
The Book of Football: A History to 1905-06	1-874287-13-9
Football's War & Peace: The Tumultuous Season of 1946-47	1-874287-70-8

TOTTENHAM HOTSPUR

Champions of England
1950-51 & 1969-61

Series Editor: Clive Leatherdale

Kevin Palmer

DESERT ISLAND BOOKS

First published in 2004
by
DESERT ISLAND BOOKS LIMITED
89 Park Street, Westcliff-on-Sea, Essex SS0 7PD
United Kingdom
www.desertislandbooks.com

© 2004 Kevin Palmer

The right of Kevin Palmer to be identified as author of this work has been asserted under The Copyright Designs and Patents Act 1988

British Library Cataloguing-in-Publication Data
A catalogue record for this book is available from the British Library

ISBN 1-874287-84-8

All rights reserved. No part of this book may be reproduced or utilised in any form or by any means, electronic or mechanical, including photocopying, recording or by any information storage and retrieval system, without prior permission in writing from the Publisher

Printed in Great Britain
by
Biddles Ltd, King's Lynn

Jacket illustrations:
1960-61 side: (Standing) Bill Brown, Peter Baker, Ron Henry
Danny Blanchflower, Maurice Norman, Dave Mackay.
(Seated) Cliff Jones, John White, Bobby Smith, Les Allen, Terry Dyson
1950-51 side: (From left) Bill Nicholson, Les Medley, Sonny Walters,
Arthur Willis, Les Duquemin, Ron Burgess, Ted Ditchburn,
Peter Murphy, Eddie Baily, unknown, Cecil Poynter (trainer).
This photo was taken after the final game
of the season v Liverpool (5th May 1951)

~ Contents ~

	Page
Author's Note	6
Preface by Tony Marchi	7
Introduction: Owls to the Sword (28th April 1951)	8
1. The Genesis of 'Push and Run' (1938-50)	10
2. Sustaining the Momentum (July-October 1950)	22
3. The Climb to the Summit (November 1950 – February 1951)	32
4. The March to the Title (March-May 1951)	45
5. The Ten-Year Itch (1951-60)	56
6. The Perfect Start (August-November 1960)	100
7. Maintaining the Pace (November 1960 – February 1961)	113
8 Achieving the Double (March-May 1961)	125
9 How the Mighty Fell (1961-77)	136
Guide to Seasonal Summaries	147
Seasonal Summaries	148
Subscribers	160

~ Author's Note ~

I hope this book is a fitting tribute to the talents of Arthur Rowe and Bill Nicholson. They remain the greatest that Tottenham Hotspur have ever produced and their achievements need shouting from the rooftops at regular intervals. The mists of time are starting to obscure them these days, and I hope a little fresh air will blow them away and allow light to shine again on those remarkable sides.

It would have been easy to cobble together bits from the dozens of books that have been written about the Spurs teams from this era, rather in the manner of a cook using the leftovers from Sunday lunch to make a stew on the Monday. Because I wanted a fresh approach I deliberately avoided reading any of these worthy tomes and concentrated on building up a picture in my own mind from other sources. Phil Soar's 1982 publication *And The Spurs Go Marching On* gave me a useful template on the history of Spurs, and this is the exception.

Most of the detail on individual matches comes from Tottenham's local newspaper the *Weekly Herald*, but I also spoke to many of the players – Tony Marchi (who provided the preface), Dennis Uphill, Les Allen and Terry Dyson were some of the heroes who helped to put a more personal slant on proceedings. Also I must thank Michael Basser and other Spurs fans who weighed in with gems from the terraces.

Nick Manning deserves some sort of award for collecting a vast collection of Spurs memorabilia and photographs, and readers can see the results for themselves. Thanks, too, for all those who originally took the photos, whoever you may be. I would thank you individually if I could.

Leigh Edwards provided the answers to numerous offbeat questions at all-too frequent intervals, whilst my wife Sharon put up with my continued absence from the living room gamely. She also helped out to fix our computer when it refused to cooperate.

Finally a big thanks to my publisher, Clive Leatherdale, for suggesting this book and putting it on the shelves; and thank you to the person reading this now. I hope you enjoy it.

Kevin Palmer

~ Preface ~

When I was a youth-team player at Spurs, manager Arthur Rowe sometimes used to let me watch the games with him in the directors box (they didn't have touchline managers in those days). He tried to explain to me his new style that came to be known as 'Push and Run', but I was too young to think in terms of systems, though I always went along with what he wanted.

I got my big break in the Division Two Championship side of 1949-50, following an injury to Bill Nicholson. I was gobsmacked to be running out onto the pitch with great players like Alf Ramsey, Ted Ditchburn and Ron Burgess. These were the heroes I'd watched from the 'Shelf' in the East Stand as a kid. With 'McNamara's Band' ringing out, the atmosphere inside White Hart Lane was terrific. I knew that as long as I did my best, the fans would be very supportive of me. There was no booing or obscenities, just cries of 'Up the Lilywhites'.

I did my National Service for two years after that, so didn't get to play in the Championship side of 1950-51, though I saw them often. I was amazed at how Arthur Rowe's system worked and how other teams were bemused by it. They were all playing a cruder, less sophisticated style, though they were still geared to attack. They were exciting times and if there weren't 60,000 in White Hart Lane we were disappointed.

I eventually went on to captain the side, though the team was ageing by then. In 1957 I was lured to Italy by the big money, but returned in 1959 at the behest of manager Bill Nicholson. By 1960-61 something had gelled, though nobody can seem to understand why. Other teams appeared frightened of us and we had so much confidence. Even so, it's only with hindsight that I can look back at how fabulous our achievements were in capturing the double, and winning England's first European trophy. I just didn't realise it at the time.

As an Edmonton boy I always felt destined to play for Spurs, and I'm proud to be the only player to be part of both Championship squads. I only hope that the current team are inspired to lift themselves back up to these heights.

Tony Marchi

Introduction

~ Owls to the Sword ~

(28th April 1951)

It was fast approaching 4pm on Saturday, 28th April 1951. Top of the table Tottenham were entertaining lowly Sheffield Wednesday in the penultimate match of the season. As was traditional in those days, it was a 3.15 kick-off. The outcome of the game was equally critical to both clubs. A win for Spurs would guarantee their first ever championship. For the Owls, a win would keep them up, a draw probably likewise, but a defeat would leave them facing the abyss of relegation to Division Two. Given the circumstances, it was a surprisingly modest crowd of 46,645 that had congregated inside White Hart Lane. That crowd now awaited the half-time whistle from referee Iliffe.

Suddenly, a typical quick-fire move from the home side. Ron Burgess – his balding figure looking much older than his 34 years – sprayed a pass out to Eddie Baily, who instinctively sensed the urgency that was required. Baily shimmied past three bemused Sheffield Wednesday players, evading them as a skier does slalom poles, and glanced up towards the penalty area. Les Medley and Len Duquemin darted in opposite directions to shake off their markers, allowing Baily to slip the ball to Medley. The Wednesday defenders converged on him, but they were too late, because Medley had already steered the ball into the path of Duquemin. The Channel Islander, affectionately known as 'The Duke', unleashed an unstoppable shot that seemed designed to test the strength of the goal nets. Mr Iliffe blew his whistle to legitimise the goal, and Spurs were well on their way to clinching their first League title.

Those in the crowd able to barge their way to the refreshment stalls to grab a hot drink – of Bovril, most likely – could sup in contentment, knowing that even if Spurs were somehow to lose this game, they still had one more – at home to Liverpool – in which to pick up the necessary two points. The Tottenham players knew the score, in all senses, but their manager Arthur Rowe told the players in the dressing room that second-placed Manchester United were winning 3-0. Tottenham could not afford to risk allowing another opportunity to go begging, because they had failed to seal the championship in their previous two matches. In short, Spurs were wobbling.

Introduction: Owls to the Sword *(28th April 1951)*

On the resumption, Tottenham gamefully tried to add another goal to settle the nerves. The Duke smacked his next effort against the goal-post. Baily cracked a fearful drive that the Wednesday goalkeeper, McIntosh, painfully saved using his face. Sonny Walters was the next in line, but he only provoked a more conventional, if much more athletic save from the Wednesday goalie.

At last the anxious expressions on the Tottenham faces turned to elation when the final whistle blew and the team was officially confirmed as the best in the land. The victorious players threw their arms round one another in joyful relief and acknowledged the diehard fans who had supported them through the mediocre Second Division seasons immediately following the War. Spurs now emulated Liverpool in 1904-06 and Everton in 1930-32, whose teams had been crowned champions of the Second and First Divisions in consecutive seasons.

The players finally left the pitch to the sanctuary of the dressing room, where they were plied with champagne. As they leaped and larked about, few spared a thought for the dejected Wednesday players who had sportingly stood and applauded the new champions from the pitch. As they trudged wearily back into their own dressing room, the Owls players were presented with a compensatory bottle of champagne for their own use. Whether any of them took a swig is unknown, because their First Division future was still in the balance. If any of the bubbly was quaffed, it might have been to dull the realisation of the fate awaiting them. Those fears came true on the final Saturday when relegation was confirmed. A draw at White Hart Lane would have kept them up.

Somewhere up amongst that happy throng in the directors box stood manager Arthur Rowe. In those days, it was trainers who frequented the dugouts, not managers. Rowe made his way down to the changing rooms, having fought off the eager masses of well-wishers and gratefully closed the door on the outside world for a few minutes. His joyous team were eager to see him, because they knew that his footballing revolution had been instrumental to their success. Rowe had perfected a system known as 'Push and Run' that was no less than the birth of modern football as we know it, with quick, incisive short-passing amongst players who were no longer shackled to the conventions of their own nominal positions.

Amongst those eleven players were two who paid particular attention to Rowe. In time, Bill Nicholson and Alf Ramsey would utilise the basic principles that he had instilled in them, and add their own ideas to create teams that were destined to conquer Europe and the World. Tottenham might only have been Champions of England twice, so far, but the legacy they have left English and World football has been immeasurable.

Chapter 1

~ THE GENESIS OF 'PUSH AND RUN' ~
(1938-50)

Even though Tottenham Hotspur are currently awaiting a third championship success to add to their 1951 and 1961 triumphs, they remain one of the biggest clubs in the country, on whatever criteria you care to judge it. Though they have been perennial bridesmaids in the League since then, they have captured five FA Cups, three League Cups, two UEFA Cups and a European Cup-Winners' Cup in that time, so they can hardly be called unsuccessful. Tottenham have been members of the top division since 1950 (apart from a seasonal aberration in 1977-78), and remain one of the most talked about League clubs in newspapers, radio and TV programmes, and in pubs up and down the land, and they continue to be amongst the best supported.

It is therefore quite difficult to cast one's mind back to 1950, and to appreciate that at that time Tottenham Hotspur were an unexceptional football club. Elected to the Football League in 1908, they had spent virtually as long in the Second Division as the First, and even on their sporadic forays amongst the elite, they had hardly shone, finishing in the top ten only twice.

Spurs did enjoy a brief golden period immediately following the First World War. They won the Second Division title in 1919-20, followed up by claiming the FA Cup in 1921, and the following season finished as runners-up in the championship, though it must be acknowledged they ended up a distant six points behind Liverpool. Thereafter, gradual but relentless decline set in. From 1928 to 1950 Spurs were permanent members of the Second Division, apart from one brief escape in 1933-35. To add to their predicament, neighbours Arsenal were rampant in the 1930s, capturing five League titles and two FA Cups. It is an understatement to say that Tottenham were living in the shadows of the Gunners; they were close to being buried by them.

Our story really begins at the beginning of the 1938-39 season, when Tottenham chairman Charles Roberts (celebrating 43 years in charge) decided it was time to axe Jack Tresarden from the manager's seat. Tresarden had failed to raise his team to anything like a promotion challenge, so Roberts decided to opt for the devil he knew, by re-appointing

Peter McWilliam as the 'new' boss. McWilliam had been in charge from 1912-27 and had kept Spurs in the top flight throughout his stewardship; apart from the one season in which he captured the Second Division championship – 1919-20. This record made him a popular choice, but obviously age was against him.

Whether Chairman Roberts was aware of the impending world war, and decided to appoint McWilliam on a caretaker basis until it burst upon us, is open to conjecture. Certainly the new manager was constrained by a poor financial situation at White Hart Lane. The building of the new East Stand in the mid-1930s had cost a crippling £60,000 at a time when the club were only occasionally showing even a modest profit. The new stand seemed like a good idea when Tottenham had rejoined the First Division in 1933 and finished third the following season, but looked more of a white elephant following relegation in 1935. There was little consolation in boasting the best stand in the Second Division.

McWilliam was therefore unable to buy his way out of the Second Division. He cast his eye over the immature players in Spurs' junior sides as he strove to replace the weaker members of his first-team squad. Lurking in the dark recesses of the club were some gems.

The only two members of Spurs' first League Championship-winning side to appear for the club before the War were Ron Burgess and Bill Nicholson. Burgess hailed from Cwm in South Wales and made a gradual progression from schoolboy football in Ebbw Vale, to appearing for his local side Cwm Villa. His performances there attracted the attention of Cardiff City, who were past their heyday and were now languishing in the bowels of Division Three (South).

Burgess remained an amateur with the Bluebirds, but he still caught the eye of Tottenham's roving scouts, ever on the lookout for cut-price talent. They persuaded him to leave Cardiff and sign amateur forms for Spurs in May 1936, shortly after his nineteenth birthday. Burgess then followed the recognised route for blossoming Tottenham talent. In April 1937 he joined Northfleet, which was utilised as a nursery club for Spurs. Northfleet is a small Kent town on the banks of the Thames estuary and its football club was located in Stonebridge Road. The club merged with its neighbours in 1946 to become Gravesend and Northfleet, but before the Second World War it gratefully nurtured the talents of up-coming stars amidst the numerous wannabe players who would never make the grade.

By the start of the 1938-39 season, Burgess had turned professional. He played in almost half the games that season at left-half, although supporters and teammates quickly got used to the idea that he could not be shackled into one position. He roved forward and frequently demolished the set formations of opposition midfields with his phenomenal turn of speed. Indeed, one of the hardest jobs for the Spurs coaches was to get the enthusiastic Burgess to race back to his defensive duties once an attack had broken down. Fortunately, the team also included the more defensively minded right-half Bill Nicholson, who apparently rated Burgess as even better than Dave Mackay, which is as high a compliment as could possibly be paid.

Nicholson hailed from Scarborough in what is now North Yorkshire, and was playing football at a casual level for the Young Liberals when he was spotted by one of Tottenham's regional scouts in 1936 and invited for a trial. Tottenham's lowly standing at this time can be gauged by the fact that Nicholson didn't even know where the place was, only that it was 'down south'. The trial was successful and he was taken on as a member of the groundstaff (which involved more sweeping, painting and cleaning than playing), before graduating to the upper echelons of life at Northfleet and turning professional at eighteen.

With so much team rebuilding going on, Tottenham weren't ready to launch a serious promotion bid, and they finished the 1938-39 season in eighth position. They might have fared better the following season, with some more promising youngsters about to emerge, but we shall never know, because after three League games had been completed, Prime Minister Neville Chamberlain gravely announced that the country was at war with Germany. Incidentally, Tottenham were lying seventh at the time, having won one and drawn two, with Burgess and Nicholson ever-presents.

It would paint an entirely false picture to read too much into Tottenham's wartime games. Though the Football League organised a 'Football League South', which Tottenham joined, so many players were called to arms, or were despatched to other parts of the country, that line-ups were unrecognisable from one match to the next. Numerous guest players from other clubs turned out for Spurs (including future England international Wilf Mannion from Middlesbrough), and the manager had to pick whoever was around to play. The Regional League South of 1940-41 is indicative of the chaos. Tottenham finished eighth in a 34-team League, but some sides only completed ten fixtures, whilst Watford managed 35. Goal-average was used to decide the table instead of points.

The principal reason for focusing on the war games is that many of the 1950-51 championship-winning side emerged then. Three future stars appeared in the Regional League South in 1939-40, namely Les Medley, Les Bennett and Ted Ditchburn.

Medley was one of a plethora of local lads who appeared for Spurs in that era, having been born in Edmonton in September 1920. His promise was apparent from an early age and he appeared for a variety of local and county school teams, before eventually reaching the dizzy heights of the England Schoolboy team. Tottenham Hotspur had already pinned him down as a future star and he moved from their Junior side to their nursery club, Northfleet, in 1935, turning professional in February 1939. Medley joined the RAF during the War and was stationed in Canada, where he turned out for the Toronto Greenbacks and Ulster United, and also had the good fortune to meet his future wife.

Les Bennett was a couple of years older than Medley, but this Wood Green lad followed a similar career path until war broke out. As well as Spurs, he also guested for Distillery, Torquay and Millwall during the years of conflict.

Ted Ditchburn was born in Gillingham in October 1921 and played in goal for Northfleet Paper Mills before joining the Spurs groundstaff in 1937. He, not surprisingly, was a stalwart for Northfleet's better-known side before the War, and was all set to become Tottenham's first-choice goalkeeper in 1940s. Ditchburn's father had been a professional boxer and his son contemplated the idea of emulating him before deciding on a life on the football pitch. The temptation to use some of these pugilistic skills against opposition forwards must have been overwhelming at times. Each of these players contributed to Tottenham's capture of the Football League South's titles in consecutive seasons between 1943-45, and by the time the War ended they had been joined by many others who would become stalwarts of the post-War era.

The cessation of hostilities came too late for the Football League to restart normally in August 1945, so the main interest centred on the FA Cup which uniquely became a two-legged affair in order to generate more action for the spectators, though a 2-4 aggregate defeat by Brentford did not disturb Spurs fans for too long. Instead, it was August 1946 when normal service was resumed. The 1946-47 fixtures replicated those of 1938-39, as Spurs attempted to escape from the Second Division.

Six survivors from the pre-War team turned out for the club that season, but the only one to be an integral part of both eras was Vic Buckingham. Many potentially great players must have been discarded during those seven years, although thankfully only a few were killed in action. Two distinguished club servants did leave during the War, though. Manager McWilliams stepped down in 1942 to make way for club secretary Arthur Turner to take the reins, whilst Chairman Roberts passed away the following year. Turner subsequently passed the managership of the club into the hands of Joe Hulme in 1946. Hulme had been a major cog in Arsenal's success in the 1930s and it was hoped that he had picked up some useful tips from their legendary manager Herbert Chapman along the way.

Five members of the coming Championship side were regulars in that first post-War Division Two outfit. Ted Ditchburn had seemingly stitched himself permanently inside his green jersey, such was his determination to hang onto his team place. In the days when, perhaps, training schedules and fitness routines were sometimes regarded as a necessary evil, rather than an essential element of a footballer's diary, Ditchburn would practice repeatedly all the skills he required. Usually the other players tired of having to flight over countless crosses or fire short-range shots, long before Ted did. Brian Clough always reckoned that Peter Shilton reduced the goals against column by a dozen over the course of a season, and no doubt the same was true of Ditchburn. Tottenham conceded 53 goals that first season, reduced that to 43 and 42 in subsequent seasons, before only letting in a miserly 35 in their promotion season. Ditchburn got better and better, and encouraged and cajoled the players around him to do the same.

Bill Nicholson and Ron Burgess re-established themselves as first-choice half-backs, with Les Bennett as inside-forward and Arthur Willis at left-back. Apart from Willis, all these players would play week in and week out for the next few years, laying down the granite foundations on which success would be built.

It was not easy for any manager in that period, because even players in their late twenties lacked League experience. Today, the names of other Spurs players might not be familiar to many, other than to the most dedicated supporter, probably advanced in years, but men like George Ludford deserve a mention. Joe Hulme somehow had to turn this motley group into a promotion-winning side, virtually from scratch.

For a while it looked promising. Spurs embarked on a twelve-match unbeaten run during the autumn of 1946, but it was a hard winter (quite literally, as it happens) and just four wins were recorded in the next sixteen games. Spurs also succumbed in the FA Cup, but there was no disgrace in losing to championship-challengers Stoke City after a replay. A better spring could not save the season. Spurs finished sixth, and of course in those days only two teams were promoted. They even finished below Chesterfield, who had enjoyed their best ever season.

1947-48 followed a similar pattern, with minor variations. A stonking 5-1 win over Sheffield Wednesday set the scene nicely, and by the end of February the local bookmakers were reluctant to take bets on Tottenham going up, as it looked assured. Tottenham had also re-established their FA Cup pedigree and recorded fairly comfortable wins over Bolton, West Brom and Leicester. Southampton had proved tougher nuts to crack in the quarter-finals, but their shell split open after a replay and Spurs were through to a semi-final tussle with Blackpool at Villa Park.

Tottenham matched their First Division opponents all the way and took the lead midway through the second half, through their new centre-forward Len Duquemin. He scrambled what the fans, bedecked in white and blue, hoped would be the winner, but their joy was short-lived. That most fearsome of post-War strikers, Stan Mortensen, single-handedly destroyed the Londoners' defence with a hat-trick. The Wembley dream was dead once again.

The aforementioned Duquemin constituted another one of Hulme's building blocks. Duquemin was born in Guernsey in July 1924 and turned out for the local schoolboy side and Vauxbelet before the Germans occupied the Channel Islands. Duquemin played for Colchester United and Chelmsford City during the war years and in 1946 had a trial with Tottenham, which led to his eventual signing.

Defeat in the FA Cup semi-final dealt a double blow to Spurs. Firstly, it shattered the players' confidence, and the 0-3 home defeat by Barnsley was an accurate reflection on how the rest of the season would go. The second problem, which had been effectively masked by the early season bravado, was the lack of goalscoring threat up front. No blame can be attached to the Duke, who weighed in with a reasonable tally of sixteen in the League, but he had no competition in Spurs' goal-getters table. Les Bennett would normally chip in with at least a dozen goals, but his tally this time was a meagre eight. Hulme had tightened the defence: now he had to simultaneously spark the attack, a difficult juggling act to achieve.

The following season (1948-49) suggested that Hulme had finally cracked it. Only four defeats had been suffered by Christmas, and four-goal winning margins had been recorded over Coventry, Chesterfield, Blackburn and Bradford Park Avenue at White Hart Lane. An early Cup exit against the dreaded Arsenal (0-3 at Highbury) was tempered by the hope that everyone could concentrate on the League, in that time-honoured footballing cliché.

It wasn't to be. Though Tottenham remained a difficult team to beat (no other team in the division lost fewer than their nine defeats that season), they foundered due to a profligacy of drawn games. The only people to benefit from this were grateful Pools punters and the two promotion teams, Fulham and West Brom. Tottenham finished fifth, six points behind salvation.

Joe Hulme had proved himself to be a 'nearly' manager. He had assembled a team that had the potential to reach the top, but he lacked the tactical nous to convert that promise into consistent success over the course of a season. He was a good judge of a player, but it takes more than a knack to spot a thoroughbred in a field of nags to be a top manager. It requires a shrewd brain to get these disparate talents working together. That proved to be the critical difference between Hulme and his successor, Arthur Rowe. Hulme had eleven great players on the pitch, but it took a footballing genius like Rowe to mould them into a genuine team who all worked together to achieve their ambitions.

Before Hulme left, he helped acquire the final two pieces of the title-winning kit though someone else was needed to assemble it. Harry Clarke joined the club in March 1949 as an old-fashioned stopper. Although hailing from Woodford (where he was born in February 1923), he 'emigrated' to Wales after the War and played for Lovell's Athletic, quaintly, a works team for a toffee manufacturers in Newport, South Wales. Though they may have been the butt of many jokes, Lovell's had the last laugh by capturing the Welsh Cup in 1948, overcoming Shrewsbury Town (then also a non-league club) 3-0. Clarke was the undoubted star of their side and the antennae of chief scout Ben Ives twitched in anticipation as he relayed news of this find to his superiors.

The other new man arrived at the end of the season, though assistant-manager Jimmy Anderson deserves the credit for this signing. In numerous Spurs games against Southampton, one opponent had stood out, right-back Alf Ramsey. In an era when full-backs were often workaday plodders, robotically going through the motions, mopping up attacks then hoofing the ball upfield, here was a player with a true footballing brain. Not content with remaining in his little corner of the field, Ramsey frequently roamed up the pitch, even venturing into the opposition half, which was as unlikely as finding a nun in a working man's club in those days. He had already earned his first England cap (in a 6-1 win over Switzerland in December 1948), alongside another international debutant, namely Ted Ditchburn (who became the first goalkeeper to usurp Frank Swift from between the sticks since the War). Though Ramsey was 29 when Tottenham signed him, he was still reckoned to have his best years ahead of him.

The new manager brought in for the start of the 1949-50 season was Arthur Rowe, but he was a familiar figure to the pre-War crowd at White Hart Lane. Rowe had played 182 League games as a centre-half in the 1930s and had already experienced promotion to the First Division as a player in 1932-33. He gained a solitary cap for England in 1934 against a

French eleven, where his unconventional roving style was much commented on. In those days, players were usually expected to stay in their allotted positions, not go gandering all over the park. It was this individuality that ensured that Rowe would come up with some unusual answers to common footballing problems.

Rowe retired from playing at the end of 1937-38, whereupon he moved to Hungary as one of several coaches to the national team. Though we would have to wait until the 1950s before the Magic Magyars ripped England apart 6-3 at Wembley and 7-1 in Budapest, it is fascinating to speculate how much of what Rowe learned in Hungary he was able to incorporate into the new 'Tottenham Style'. Certainly the Ferenc Puskas-dominated Hungarians of the 1950s lifted footballing tactics onto another planet, compared with the crudity employed by most English sides, but it was Rowe who first injected some of those ideas into English football, though it must be stressed, in a much simpler form.

The imminent threat of war saw Rowe beat a hasty retreat to his homeland, at a time when he had become a strong candidate for becoming Hungary's new national coach. That thought is enough to provoke another discussion beginning with the words 'What if?' What a prospect it would have been to witness the Hungarians trouncing the self-proclaimed 'Masters of Football', with the very English Arthur Rowe at the helm. Anyway, the War ensured that this was just a pipe dream, and Rowe did his bit for the war effort by keeping the troops fit and entertained, like so many of his fellow footballers.

After the War, Southern League Chelmsford City were astute enough to employ Rowe in his first managerial role. The Essex side had only been formed in 1938, but had gained prominence in their first season by crushing Second Division Southampton 4-1 in the third round of the FA Cup, despite their lowly Southern League placing. With Rowe in charge, they carried on where they left off, and in his first full season (1945-46) they claimed the double of Southern League and Southern League Cup. They were then runners-up in the Southern League in 1948-49, so it was hardly surprising that Tottenham were first in line to whisk him into Football League management when he took charge on 4th May 1949.

The side that Rowe was to carry to such heights was already waiting for him, with the exception of Sid McClellan, who came with him from New Whittle Street. Although quite experienced, the Spurs team's footballing education was just about to begin.

The 'Push and Run' system that Rowe developed was born on a train returning from Bradford in the 1930s. One of Spurs' goals that day had excited the centre-half, because it had consisted of a string of passes stretching from one end of the pitch to the other. Although the goal had come about almost by coincidence, it set the player pondering. Surely, if the players on the pitch concentrated on passing to the man nearest to them, and if the men not in possession were to move into positions where they could receive the ball, then more success would follow more often? Up until then, even the top sides relied heavily on their players giving an almighty hoof from one end of the pitch to the other, and it was largely a lottery if a teammate received the ball. Rowe's idea was to reduce the odds of that lottery and turn it into a dead-cert.

No doubt his time in Hungary had given him opportunity to experiment, and Chelmsford enabled him to implement his blackboard plans on the pitch. Now, at Spurs, he at last had the personnel blessed with the ability to take these tactics and dazzle the whole of England.

So what was this system that became known as 'Push and Run?' For a start, Rowe didn't like that term, thinking it too crude, although he never came up with a better tag himself. The genesis of the system came from schoolboy games in the streets. With the absence of proper pitches, balls would frequently be played with the outside of the boot against a convenient kerb or wall. The ball would bounce off the immovable object, effectively bypassing the opponent. The static object would thus become an extra 'man' for your team. Rowe's idea was to use players instead of walls. If a player could lay the ball off first time back to the instigator of the move, opposition players could be swept aside without needing to run the risk of being tackled. This 'one-two' or 'triangle' method was well-known in football, though it had never previously been employed on so grand a scale. The system relied on those players without the ball moving into the best position to receive it. The beauty of the plan was that that it didn't matter if the player about to take possession was marked, because if he released the ball instantly, the marking player wouldn't have time to make the tackle.

This meant that two long-held footballing beliefs were consigned to the Spurs dustbin. Ted Ditchburn was no longer expected to punt goalkicks as far as possible, but instead throw the ball out to a full-back to commence an attack. This was practical in more ways than one, as Ditchburn was a hopeless kicker of the ball and was more inclined to throw the ball out anyway. The second 'take-it-as-read' command to be jettisoned was the rigid positioning of the men on the pitch. Previously, full-backs were expected to stay in their own half, whilst the winger ahead of them was supposed to reside in the opposition half. Rowe encouraged every player to put himself in whichever half the action was taking place, and even to switch positions temporarily if the occasion demanded. By giving players more positional freedom, it guaranteed confusion amongst the opposition ranks. The opposing left-back might be detailed to mark Sonny Walters on the wing, but would not know how to cope with the sight of Alf Ramsey haring forward alongside him in support. Because players were inclined to pop up in unusual positions, it encouraged a more varied supply of balls to be delivered to the goal-getters. Now players were expected to use their grey matter, but paradoxically it meant that more teamwork was displayed than under more conventional systems, where individual dribbling talents were more highly prized.

It might be thought that Rowe would be a rigid disciplinarian, forcing his systems and ideas onto his men and banning them from trying to play any other way, but that is not the case. Rowe as a player was unconventional. He was apt to try things out on the spur of the moment, and this spontaneity was transferred into his coaching methods. He talked through his ideas, demonstrating his methods on the training pitch, then allowing the players to try things out for themselves. The men may have been initially slightly baffled by such thinking, but Rowe's patience and enthusiasm made coaching and training fun. With eleven men on the pitch eager to play the Rowe way, not coerced into it, there was far more likelihood of ensuing success.

One aspect of the new system easily forgotten is the extra physical demands imposed. Instead of patrolling their own patch and waiting for balls to come, players found themselves sprinting up and down the pitch, actively seeking it. Tottenham players needed to be super fit. Training sessions were held at Cheshunt, Hertfordshire, less than ten miles north of White Hart Lane. For most clubs, training sessions consisted of lots of running, with very little heed paid to ball work. Indeed, many clubs never used a ball at all during training, on the theory that it would make the players 'hungry' for the ball on the Saturday. Rowe reckoned that employing his methods would ensure that the players would not even recognise the ball by the time Saturday came around.

Although Arthur Rowe was always present at these sessions, he was not a 'tracksuit manager' and preferred to let trainers do the donkey work with the players. Instead he concentrated on imparting his theories and ideas to them in informal discussions. This ensured that training was always interesting and varied. Although the players were still conditioned to a physical peak, this has to be judged by the standards of the time. Even amongst professional players there were many who smoked and drank heavily as part of their normal routine. Ignorance about diet meant that a chunky steak was often consumed a couple of hours before a game.

Rowe's first match in charge was at Brentford. 'Push and Run' brought instant success as Spurs cruised to a 4-1 victory. Tottenham's Second Division opponents had no idea what was happening to them, let alone any plans as to how to counter it, and they crumbled under the relentless attacks. Using wartime analogies, it was something akin to the way the Germans had blitzkrieged their way through Europe in 1940. Spurs' opening 25 League matches – up until New Year's Eve 1949 – resulted in twenty wins, four draws, and one defeat (at home to Blackburn on 27th August). The Second Division championship race was virtually over, with Spurs leaving a wake of shell-shocked teams at least ten points behind them. Sheffield United visited White Hart Lane on 12th November as one of the fancied teams for promotion and were imperiously swept aside 7-0. The revolution had begun.

The FA Cup odyssey started in January and enabled Rowe to try out his system against top drawer opposition. 'Push and Run' had annihilated most teams' conventional systems, but would it come unstuck against the more-organised and better class of opponents found in the First Division? The answer was an emphatic no! Stoke were elbowed aside at the Victoria Ground in the third round, whilst championship-contenders Sunderland were thrashed 5-1 at White Hart Lane, unable to cope with attacks that seemed to swamp them from all imaginable angles, and quite a few unimaginable ones.

Alas for Spurs, it was they who were victims in the fifth round, punished by Everton at Goodison Park. Tottenham claimed to be innocent of the offence, but the referee found Harry Clarke guilty of handball in the penalty area, and Wainwright carried out the sentence by dispatching the killer penalty. Rowe's take on the FA Cup was that they had been beaten by the worst, yet thrashed the best. He thought the victory over Sunderland had flattered Spurs by about three goals, whilst the Everton defeat had flattered the opposition by about six!

The Cup disappointment did not derail the promotion charge and Tottenham carried on before in the League, stretching the gap over the second-placed side at one stage to thirteen points. Promotion was assured with plenty of matches in hand, and the Second Division title was secured soon afterwards. The Lilywhites (Tottenham's nickname at the time) then eased off the gas and only picked up one point in their last five games, which meant they only finished a mere nine points clear of Sheffield Wednesday. Spurs' all-round dominance can also be gauged by the fact that their attack bagged 81 goals and the defence only conceded 35, both figures outstripping those of any other team. Goals came from everywhere, as was borne out by the statistics. Les Medley (winger) led the way with eighteen goals, followed by centre-forward Len Duquemin on sixteen, and inside-forward Les Bennett and winger Sonny Walters on fourteen. Just who were opposition defenders supposed to mark?

This success also meant international honours flowed Spurs's way. Eddie Baily made his international debut for England against Spain at the end of the season, joining Ditchburn and Ramsey who were rapidly becoming established. Medley and Nicholson swelled their ranks and even Harry Clarke later won a cap. Burgess was a regular No 6 for Wales, his huge balding frame making him look like a pre-War relic, even if his assured performances belied this cruel jibe.

The other gratifying fact, in the eyes of Spurs accountants, was the return of vast crowds to White Hart Lane. It was the peak era for attendances generally, and Tottenham's exciting style and outrageous success led to swarms of occasional and born-again fans to descend on Tottenham High Road. Over 70,000 witnessed the 4-0 thumping of Southampton in February, whilst the average League attendance that season was 54,405, 3,000 more than neighbours Arsenal. Tottenham were now the best-supported club in the land.

This brought problems as well as revenue to the club. The Burnden Park tragedy of 1946 was still fresh in everyone's memory – crush barriers had collapsed, killing 33 and injuring 400. White Hart Lane had now installed automatic turnstile machines to allow the monitoring of numbers in each section and, it was hoped, avoid a repetition of a potentially dangerous crush that sometimes occurred in the north-east corner of the ground. Sections would now be penned off and closed when full by 'crowd marshals' (the forerunners of safety stewards). The ground also had a 'children's section', though one parent was angered by the fact that 'great big louts' were encroaching into the kiddies corner.

The newest part of the ground was the East Stand, which accommodated 15,000 and also housed 'The Shelf', which contained the most vocal elements of Tottenham's support. The stand still looked modern in the 1970s but most First Division grounds were still using older stands even then. Not surprisingly, the old-fashioned structure facing it was billed as the West Stand and this looked small and dowdy in comparison until a new stand was completed in 1982. The North Stand was better known as the Paxton Road End, whilst the area behind the opposite goal was the Park Lane End where visiting supporters would congregate.

Everyone was eager for the new season, not least Rowe, who stated: 'I hope for a lot and expect a little. I expect we shall finish in the top half of the table. That is, in my view, a sound and common-sense valuation of our chances.' His caution is amusing in the light of what happened.

Chapter 2

~ Sustaining the Momentum ~

(July-October 1950)

The season kicked off with a home fixture against Blackpool. Although the Tangerines of the immediate post-War era have today acquired a legendary status, this is almost wholly due to the 1953 FA Cup final victory over Bolton, which was hyped as the 'Matthews final'. Stanley's quest for a winner's medal seemed to matter more to the public at large than the gentleman concerned, but the fact that the final lived up to its billing hides one rather important fact. The Blackpool side weren't actually that good. Matthews had joined them from Stoke in 1947, since when the highest finished they had attained was seventh in 1949-50. In truth, they were a team that relied heavily on their stars, Matthews on the right wing and centre-forward Stan Mortensen being the obvious examples. This is perhaps what made them more suited to Cup football than the unremitting consistency required for 42-match League football. With a system geared for supplying balls to Matthews, then for the jinking maestro to feed the forwards, the top sides had already worked out a method of staunching the flow of danger balls. But Tottenham hadn't. Although Matthews had the ability to wreak havoc with a few meagre scraps, Spurs generously permitted delivery of top-quality produce, which the master was able to turn into goals on a plate for the inrushing half-backs. Spurs' 1-4 defeat stung Arthur Rowe and shattered thoughts that his team might sweep all before it.

Tottenham put matters rights in the trip to Bolton two days later, when the Trotters were humbled by the same scoreline of 1-4. Rowe's new signing from Coventry – Peter Murphy – took the place of Les Bennett and celebrated by claiming the opening goal. That marvellous victory was conveyed to the many Spurs fans who could not make the arduous journey to Lancashire, and who were attending the home reserve match against Swindon. A board was held aloft every fifteen minutes announcing the latest score, which gladdened the hearts of the faithful who just could not afford the money or the time for long away trips. The reserves were also enjoying a productive Monday afternoon, notching a 9-0 win against Swindon reserves, with six different players getting on the scoresheet. That result was a quick response to a 1-2 defeat at Swindon on the Saturday in the opening game of the Football Combination's fixture list.

The following Saturday's game was the one that the whole of north London's footballing fraternity were yearning for. Arsenal hosted the first north London derby game in the First Division since 1934-35, when Herbert Chapman's awesome Gunners had destroyed relegation-bound Spurs 1-5 at Highbury and 0-6 at White Hart Lane. Since then, there had only been the wartime meetings in the London League and Football League South, and an FA Cup third-round tie at Highbury in January 1949 that had also gone Arsenal's way (0-3).

The renewal of old hostilities provided a fascinating clash of styles as Arthur Rowe's perfected 'push and run' came up against the famous old Arsenal tactics. The Gunners had dominated football in the 1930s with League Championships heading their way in four out of five seasons between 1930 and 1935. Although Chapman had died in 1934, his presence still seemed to be interwoven in the Arsenal side of the early 1950s. Like Rowe was about to do at Tottenham, Chapman had come up with an entirely new way of countering a footballing problem that had baffled other clubs. In Chapman's case it was the change in the offside laws in 1925 that sparked his clever system. Prior to that, teams could defend in numbers, as a player was deemed offside with three defenders between him and the goal. When that was reduced to two, in a bid to encourage more attacking play, Chapman was among the pioneers of change, bolstering his defence by introducing a custom-made centre-back. He set his Huddersfield side on course for three consecutive championships, then joined Arsenal and perfected his technique. His defensive techniques reduced the average numbers of goals conceded by top sides from about 1½ goals per game to about one – a huge difference. Not that Chapman was ultra-defensive. He also pioneered an attacking system that sprayed out long balls to either wing or straight down the middle, as opposed to the excessive dribbling that some teams persisted with. Although the current Arsenal manager, Tom Whittaker, had tinkered with the style, it was still recognisably the old Arsenal.

The keenness with which the game captured the public's imagination meant all-night queues for the guarantee of a ticket, but perhaps the expectation of the gates being locked early kept many casual fans away, because the attendance was only 64,500, some way short of the anticipated 70,000. The game started with Spurs on top, but Duquemin and Medley failed to put away good chances midway through the first half. That waywardness was punished when Arsenal's Roper sent over a cross that dipped and swerved in the wind and evaded Ditchburn's desperate leap. For the poor goalie it was an action replay of a goal conceded in the FA Cup-tie two seasons earlier. Spurs hit back quickly, though, as Ramsey placed a free-kick onto Burgess's forehead for the equaliser. The contrast in styles was amply illustrated with a classic quick-passing set of manoeuvres early in the second half that bamboozled the Gunners' defence and led to Walters giving Spurs the lead. But naivety gave the home side their equaliser. Ditchburn was about to collect the ball from a failed Arsenal attack when Lishman was brought down for a penalty which Walley Barnes gratefully dispatched. Despite this, a 2-2 draw was a satisfactory result for Spurs against the championship favourites. Tottenham's overall record against their rivals in League and Cup games remained at thirteen wins to ten in Tottenham's favour, with seven draws.

Until recent times League fixtures were arranged so that one club was faced twice, home and away, customarily the second and fourth games of the season. In 1950-51 those opponents were Bolton. Given the 4-1 win at Burnden Park, the return fixture was expected to be a walkover, but there was a nasty shock in store when Bolton raced into a two-goal lead. Both goals were created by Langton and put away by Scottish international Willie Moir. Rowe must have looked pained as Spurs then started to carve openings through the Trotters' defence but failed to convert their chances. But it was only a matter of time. Bolton's defence was unable to withstand the speed and variety of these attacks, and despite the chances that went begging, Spurs were able to convert four of them to post a comfortable victory.

A visit to Charlton's vast Valley Ground was next. It presented a tricky fixture because the Valiants had only dropped one point from their opening three games. It proved to be another game in which Spurs failed to get their forward line operating efficiency, though this time the cause was attributable to a resolute Addicks defence, rather than any waywardness in Spurs' shooting. Indeed, it took a Ramsey penalty to give the visitors the lead, but this was wiped out when Vaughan gave Charlton a deserved equaliser, just as the backroom boys were brewing the half-time tea. At least there were no problems incurred in the Tottenham defence and the match ended with no further goals being scored.

The tough opening sequence of matches continued with a Wednesday visit to Anfield, home of the 1950 FA Cup runners-up – Liverpool. In those pre-floodlight times, midweek games meant afternoon kick-offs. Floodlights were still a futuristic concept, not least because of an FA ban on artificial lighting. Indeed, it was Tottenham reserves who took part in the first competitive floodlit fixture in Britain, when Southampton played host to them at The Dell in October 1951.

It was certainly a dark and gloomy atmosphere for the few Spurs fans who made the journey to Anfield, as Liverpool emerged as 2-1 winners. The Lilywhites hadn't won there since 1912, a sequence that was set to continue until 1993.

With the opening phase of the season concluded, it would be Saturday fixtures from here on, apart from Christmas and Easter. The only exceptions were the occasional friendlies, FA Cup replays, and postponed matches. The lack of floodlights, as winter approached, was obviously the major reason for focusing on Saturdays, but with a fixture list free of minor cup competitions, European ties and the like, players were generally able to play every match if required without their managers considering anything as fancy as squad rotation. The top sides, such as Arsenal, could easily afford big squads, with a strong reserve side to provide cover for injuries and out-of-form players.

Tottenham's reserves were not particularly strong at the time, and that lack of cover was one of the most urgent problems needing attention from assistant manager Jimmy Anderson and his boss Arthur Rowe. With overall attendances in the First Division around the 40 million mark, there was no financial need to further encumber fixture list. To put this into perspective, attendances in the top flight dropped to below seventeen million in the mid-1980s, before rising towards 30 million with the renaissance of football in the new millennium. In 1950, with players' wages capped by the maximum wage of £9 per week and the barest minimum spent on ground upkeep, most football clubs were able to stay solvent with little problem. Tottenham were turning in a modest profit around this time, funded by admission prices to the terraces of one shilling (5p). Season ticket holders with seats were paying either five or six guineas for the privilege, which equates to £5.25 and £6.30 in decimal currency. In those days, clubs split their gate receipts with their opponents. Kick-off time in late spring, summer and early autumn was 3.15pm, the extra fifteen minutes presumably allowing an extra few hundred souls to rush from their Saturday jobs or watering holes to clank through the turnstiles. When the days shortened as autumn progressed, kick-off times were brought forward at fifteen-minute intervals, so that by late November onwards games started at 2.15pm.

On 9th September, Manchester United paid a visit to White Hart Lane for a First Division match. United were one of the most powerful of the post-War clubs, but had finished as First Division runners-up three seasons running between 1946-47 and 1948-49. In 1949-50 they had slipped to fourth, but even so this was another benchmark by which Spurs could judge their progress. They passed the test. Ramsey, Burgess and Nicholson were the masters of their rear 'third' of the pitch, whilst at the other end Walters poached the winning goal by firing a shot through the legs of Aston, which hoodwinked the unsighted Allen in the visitors' goal. Critics grumbled that the attack was still not firing on all cylinders. Bennett was thought to be out of touch, whilst Duquemin's lack of pace was also attracting criticism. The front line had consistently squandered goalscoring chances and this was blamed for the club's unspectacular League position, just above halfway. The lack of strength in depth, noted earlier, meant Rowe only had limited options in changing his set-up, especially when the players brought in, or reassigned to other tasks, generally did worse than the originals.

The indifferent start to the season was exemplified in the next game, at Wolverhampton. The Old Gold team seized an early advantage, and inspired by it, their forwards had a crack at goal whenever they got within shooting range. Ted Ditchburn found himself at the business end of this shooting gallery and flung himself in all directions in a valiant effort to keep the scoreline down. He distinguished himself as Wolves only won 2-1, and the applause Ted gathered from all corners of the ground once again highlighted the paucity at the other end, where the 'Duke' was having a nightmare. He seemed to dwell on the ball too long and was often dispossessed. Any thoughts at this stage that Spurs might be championship material would have been laughed at in the schoolyard or workplace, especially by smug Arsenal fans, who would have been full of themselves after their team stuffed Huddersfield 6-2 at Highbury.

Arthur Rowe provided a welcome distraction for his players, when on the Monday they fulfilled a long-standing arrangement to play a friendly against the Welsh toffee-making works team of Lovell's Athletic. Spurs had signed Harry Clarke from them in March 1949 and this was a pleasant way to say thank you and provide Athletic with a bit of extra revenue. The match kicked off at 5.45pm and gave the Spurs manager a chance to blood a couple of reserves in the first team. One such player was Tommy Harmer, a promising ball player, but considered too dainty to be thrust into the hurly-burly of League football. As much attention was paid to building up his body strength as to enhancing his ball-playing ability. Against Lovell's, Rowe noted his enthusiasm and ability and made a mental note to maybe give him a run out next season. At least young Harmer had the satisfaction of seeing his name on the scoresheet as his side banged eight goals without reply past their opponents. The other scorers were Duquemin (with a welcome hat-trick), Scarth (who was usually to be spotted tearing up the right wing for the 'A' team, but who cut inside to bag himself a brace in this game), Medley and Burgess.

Sustaining the Momentum *(July-October 1950)*

Tottenham had a good relationship with the lower-league sides nearby, as many of their players had been plucked from these outfits in the past. Nursery clubs were very much in vogue, and Northfleet was renowned as the place where future Lilywhites could be tried and tested. Just recently, Spurs had added Hoddesdon as another nursery ground, and had arranged for the Hertfordshire side to play host to some of Tottenham's 'A' games in the Eastern Counties League. Coincidentally, Hoddesdon were also nicknamed the Lilywhites.

Arthur Rowe's experimentation in the Lovell's friendly led to him trying out a couple of new boys for the home game with Sunderland on 23rd September. Not only were the first team in need of a minor shake-up, but seven players were carrying niggling injuries, so some short-term fixes were required. Duquemin was relegated to the reserves as punishment for his loss of League form and 23-year-old Sid McClellan stepped up to take his place as centre-forward. The other newcomer was Dennis Uphill, who successfully obtained leave from the Army for this game as he was in the midst of his National Service. The teenager played at inside-right. Despite fielding a couple of rookies, Tottenham were confident. After all, memories of last season's 5-1 FA Cup win were still fresh in everyone's mind.

For McClellan, his joy at making the first team was short-lived. After twenty minutes he challenged for a ball with the Rokerite centre-half, Walsh, and there a sickening clash of heads. Walsh was able to resume some time later after receiving treatment, but poor old Sid was rushed to hospital with a badly-cut chin and concussion. In those pre-substitute days the game proceeded briefly as ten-a-side, and during this time Spurs took the lead. The other new boy, Uphill, wove his way through the Sunderland defence, slipped the ball to Baily, whose shot was turned into his own goal by defender Wright. When Walsh returned, Sunderland had a man advantage for the remaining 70 minutes and equalised through Ivor Broadis, whom the north-eastern club had signed from Tottenham. Uphill, though delighted to have had an 'assist' in the goal, generally found the game chaotic. It was played at a far quicker pace than he was used to in the reserves, and he found it difficult to adjust.

Despite dropping another point, Tottenham reduced the gap with rivals Arsenal to four points after the Gunners were beaten 1-2 at leaders Newcastle.

A visit to Villa Park gave Arthur Rowe's team a chance to improve on their poor away form, which had dragged the side down to mid-table. Since the 4-1 victory at beleaguered Bolton in August, Spurs had slowly regressed with two draws and two defeats. Their chances of improving on that record seemed bleak as Burgess suffered an injury early on and was shunted out to the left wing. That was the time-honoured position for crocked players, who were cruelly labelled 'passengers' and were required to do the best they could in their remote location on the pitch. This necessitated a shuffling of positions for the others. Medley became an inside-right, whilst Murphy switched to left-half.

The genius of Rowe's system meant that players were better able than those at other clubs to adapt to a new position, because they acted not so much as a collection of individuals as parts of an efficient machine. They soon learned what was required of them, which for the positions in the middle third of the pitch was less individualistic than could be found at any other club. Murphy was able to threaten Villa from his deeper position, and it was he who let rip from 25 yards to open the scoring. Though the Villains fought back to take the lead, the team in white and blue knuckled down and won the game 3-2. The winning goal came from the restored and rejuvenated Duquemin, latching on to Medley's inch-perfect pass.

Many Tottenham supporters would have been satisfied with their club's position, safely nestled just above halfway in the table. Spurs' track record in the First Division was not encouraging, as they had finished in the top half only three times out of sixteen attempts, and the last of these was way back in 1921-22 when they had finished runners-up. It was not surprising that nobody really regarded Spurs as natural contenders for the title, and very few would seriously have tipped them for the top even at this stage. The team had safely negotiated some tough fixtures though, and October would be a kind month for them, with ample opportunity for them to ascend the table. If Spurs could not pick up a hatful of points now, then they had no right to proclaim themselves as serious challengers for the title.

The first of those October games was at home to Burnley, who were looking anxiously at the few teams below them. Spurs were handicapped by having two players picked for England in a Home International against Northern Ireland in Belfast. Alf Ramsey had been first-choice right-back for his country since November 1949, against Italy at White Hart Lane. This was his eighth consecutive appearance in the No 2 shirt. His international career had not got off to a great start, however. His debut had been in December 1948, whilst still a Southampton player, but four different right-backs had been tried in his position before he was able to reclaim, and retain, his spot.

The second Spurs player in the England eleven was Eddie Baily. He was winning his second cap, the first having come in the 1950 World Cup finals against Spain, when England were eliminated following their 0-1 defeat. Baily, however, had done enough to impress the England selectors in that game and he now repaid their faith by scoring twice in the 4-1 victory over Northern Ireland.

Sid Tickridge was a fine stand-in for Ramsey at right-back, and with Arthur Willis operating at left-back, the rearguard seemed as strong as ever. There was good service from the wings, with Medley and Walters terrorising the Burnley full-backs, and it was these two who combined for the only goal just after the half-time break, Medley stealing inside to get on the end of the right-winger's cross.

There were still problems up front for Rowe to sort out. Baily was sorely missed, and Murphy, Duquemin and Bennett seemed unsure of what to do and were lacking in confidence. Bennett in particular came in for strong criticism from 'Concord' – the football reporter on the *Weekly Herald* – for his 'irritating habit of running back, which held up the line'. Bennett was so disillusioned with life that he apparently put in a transfer request, which Rowe promptly rejected. The manager had far more belief in his inside-right than Bennett seemed to have in himself.

With eleven League games gone there was now opportunity to see how the teams were faring after the first quarter of the season. The table looked like this:

	P	W	D	L	F	A	Pts
Arsenal	12	7	3	2	24	11	17
Middlesbrough	12	8	1	3	32	16	17
Manchester U	12	7	2	3	15	7	16
Newcastle	12	5	6	1	18	10	16
Liverpool	11	5	3	3	17	12	13
Blackpool	12	4	5	3	19	14	13
SPURS	11	5	3	3	20	17	13

Nobody was very surprised to see Arsenal on top of the pile. The big eye-opener was that Middlesbrough were challenging them so gamely. Boro weren't used to reaching such lofty heights, even with the incomparable Wilf 'Golden Boy' Mannion in their side. Tottenham were nicely placed, but it tended to take a long time to overhaul four-point deficits against the top sides in those two-points-for-a-win days. Spurs were helped by having a game in hand over most of the sides above them.

Two points were confidently expected from the visit to Stamford Bridge, because Chelsea were propping up the table. This prediction duly came true, but dogged defending kept Chelsea in the frame for nearly an hour, before their defensive frailties enabled Spurs to sink them with two quick goals. Once again the attackers failed to convince, and Alex Wright must have been confident of breaking into the team, as he scored twice in the reserves' 4-0 win over Bristol City. Poor Bennett had another off-day and this led to a peculiar letter being delivered to Tottenham's offices at 748 High Road. It was apparently from Wood Green Town FC and offered to take Bennett from Spurs in exchange for two of Wood Green's best players. The letter was signed 'J.T. Rist', the secretary of Wood Green, but it did not take much investigating to reveal that the letter was a hoax. Mr Rist assured Tottenham that his club did not have any such intentions and that the letter was a 'deliberate attempt to create bad blood between the two clubs', though it seems more likely to have created mild amusement than any lingering resentment.

Arsenal were still marching onwards, having dispatched championship pretenders Manchester United 3-0 at Highbury and gained a point at Aston Villa on 21st October, but they were now being lined up in the gun-sights of their nearest London neighbours. For the first time this season, Spurs really turned on the style, routing Stoke City 6-1. The confidence gleaned from three straight wins had permeated through to the front line, who ripped apart a goodish Stoke side with ease. It was especially pleasing for Rowe to see his much-maligned duo of Duquemin and Bennett grab a brace of goals apiece. The push and run system had now proved its worth at the highest level and Rowe was able to state boldly that the games were becoming easier for his team as they rose steadily up the table. He was also delighted that his team had turned it on at White Hart Lane, and now had equalled the fourteen-goal haul that they had earned on their travels. It had been a minor mystery to the boss why his side had been scoring freely away from north London, but any attacking system is more likely to pay dividends on a team's travels, where opponents are less likely to be defensive minded.

On a sadder note, George Cox resigned from the board for health reasons, but nobody could really blame him for wanting to take life easier in his 95th year! He had become a director in 1902, the year after Spurs' first FA Cup triumph, and a full six years before they emerged from the Southern League into the more rarefied atmosphere of the Football League. Mr Bearman, son of the chairman, replaced him.

West Bromwich Albion were the hosts for Spurs' next match on 28th October. The middling Midlanders played their part in a great game, but Tottenham's back line was able to absorb the Baggies' initial onslaught and strike back to open the scoring through a well-worked free-kick routine. Willis floated the ball over the defenders and Walters nipped through to head the ball into the net. Medley made it 2-0 after Baily had sidestepped his would-be tacklers, and this gave Spurs the cushion to hang on, despite the home side pulling a goal back. For Spurs it was the third season in a row that they had gone through October unbeaten. They were now up to fifth, three points behind Arsenal and Newcastle, and a point below Middlesbrough who had hit a wobbly patch.

	P	W	D	L	F	A	Pts
Arsenal	15	9	4	2	31	13	22
Newcastle	15	8	6	1	27	13	22
Middlesbrough	15	8	4	3	34	18	20
Manchester U	15	8	3	4	19	11	19
SPURS	14	8	3	3	30	19	19
Wolves	14	7	3	4	32	21	17

Chapter 3

~ THE CLIMB TO THE SUMMIT ~

(November 1950 – February 1951)

A fitting examination for the new title claimants was a home game against the defending club from the two previous seasons. Portsmouth had assembled a fine team with largely home-grown talent. The absence of big-name players set something of an example to clubs like Tottenham, who were hoping to muscle in. Spurs had reason for optimism because Pompey were an aging side which already looked doomed to relinquishing their title. They were down in eleventh place, eight points adrift of the pacesetters. Pompey were further handicapped by injuries that meant three reserve-team players took to the field. They were particularly weak on their right flank, and Medley and Baily were able to launch a myriad of attacks using this channel. Any Pompey chimes escaping into the autumn breeze at White Hart Lane were merely announcing the death of their great side, as they passed their mantle over to the new pretenders to the throne. Baily mustered his first senior hat-trick, and to rub Portsmouth's noses into it further, their consolation goal in the 5-1 drubbing was gifted to them by Willis, whose 'back pass' to Ditchburn metamorphosed into a blistering shot.

Tottenham's reserves had battled to the semi-finals of the London Challenge Cup, but succumbed 2-3 in extra-time in the replay against Brentford, who fielded their first team in both games. That Spurs reserves were almost the equal of a useful Second Division side shows that the club was starting to show some true strength in depth. Ron Reynolds was a regular in goal, waiting patiently for a chance to snatch Ditchburn's place. Sid Tickridge was an able deputy for Ramsey at right-back, whilst Peter Murphy had also demonstrated his usefulness in the first team. The renaissance of the forwards had also frustrated Alex Wright, who felt he should have been a regular in the first team. Jimmy Scarth and Tony Marchi had also featured in the first team at some time or other and were itching to get back into the frame, although the latter was hampered by having to do his National Service. Whilst Spurs could hardly claim that they had a top-class replacement for every position in the side, they were at least able to field a strong line-up for every game, with some juggling of roles from the master tactician Arthur Rowe.

The Climb to the Summit *(November 1950 – February 1951)*

Another distraction for Harry Clarke, Sonny Walters and Dennis Uphill was a fixture between an FA representative XI and the Army. Clarke and Walters were appearing on behalf of the FA, whilst young Uphill was an Army man, on account of his National Service. This two-year distraction of compulsory Army service caused headaches for all managers, but the Second World War had only ended five years earlier, and the world was still unstable with the onset of the Cold War. This was highlighted in June 1950 with the outbreak of the Korean War, which saw a sizeable contingent of British troops heading East to shore up South Korea's defences. For a long while to come, Army life was destined to become an integral part of most young men's early careers, for National Service would not be discontinued until the early 1960s. For some wayward youngsters, military discipline could not come soon enough: a small band of Spurs hooligans had thrown missiles from within the juvenile enclosure. The directors threatened to close the section off, if this bad behaviour didn't cease forthwith. Thankfully it did.

As if this game was not enough to provide some variety, Spurs also played a couple of matches against the university sides of Cambridge and Oxford. Half the first team went to each venue, with Vic Buckingham coaching the Oxford players and Bill Nicholson performing a similar role at Cambridge. Spurs achieved a 2-1 win over Cambridge, whilst their other halves drew 1-1 at Oxford.

Two days later, on 11th November, attention was firmly directed back towards the League championship with a trip to Everton. The Toffeemen found themselves in the unusual position of propping up the division, but they didn't play like a Second Division side in waiting. Spurs were on the back foot for most of the match and the fact that they still won 2-1 gave a further example of passing a test that all aspirant champions have to pass – winning a game whilst being outplayed. Hero of the day was Ted Ditchburn who was only beaten by a cruel deflection, and who preserved the two points with a breathtaking save in the closing moments, from an effort that had seemed destined to provide Everton with an equaliser.

The appearance of Newcastle at White Hart Lane was an even bigger test. The Magpies were in second place, with an away record that read: won four, drawn four and lost one. They had only conceded eight goals in those nine away games, and Spurs needed to win in order to leapfrog the Geordies into second place, depending on how Middlesbrough fared. The excitement of such a monumental clash sparked enormous interest in north London. The crowds at White Hart Lane had fluctuated between 45,000 and 65,000 for the previous home games, and now the casual supporter and interested bystanders were clamouring for admittance to see what all the fuss was about. Just over 70,000 squeezed into White Hart Lane, and that was still some 5,000 shy of the record set for the FA Cup quarter-final with Sunderland in 1938.

Of those attending the Newcastle game, 9,500 would have been seated, with about 50,000 standing under cover. Such huge attendances made life physically uncomfortable for spectators, as there was literally no room for manoeuvre. Any excitement, such as a goal being scored, would unleash surges in which the terraces swayed forward as one giant body, with each individual compelled to go with the flow. If anyone was to lose their footing in these circumstances, there was a great risk of them being trampled under the weight of the pack. Mercifully, there were no fences at the front of the terraces that proved so fatal at Hillsborough in 1989, but anyone standing against the back walls was in potential danger of being crushed as the crowd swayed back against them. Anyone who needed to reach the safety of the pitch perimeter would be passed above the heads of the fans before their feet touched the ground again.

Amazingly there were very few deaths at British grounds during those days of huge attendances, with only the Burnden Park, Bolton, tragedy of 1946 fresh in people's minds. Yet the threat remained grave, as only a minimum of preventative measures had been taken, such as the use of crush barriers to interrupt the surges. The vast crowds meant that Spurs employed 'packers' until the end of the current season to ensure as many people as possible were fed into each section without undue danger of any serious crushes developing.

The 70,000 fans witnessed a turning point in the English game's history: the whole country now realised that Rowe's 'push and run' wasn't some passing fad, but a revolution in the making. Newcastle, one of the top sides in the country, were overwhelmed as Tottenham's intricate passing was at last allied to sensational off-the-ball support and dazzling finishing. Poor Newcastle were obliterated to the tune of 7-0 and some wondered whether a finer display had ever been seen in British club football. The first goal encapsulated the Spurs style. Duquemin collected a loose ball in midfield, beat his marker, and then laid it off to Baily. Meanwhile, Medley slipped inside and Baily was able to stroke the ball into his path. Baily sensed the possibilities and now hared off down the left wing to collect Medley's raking pass. Baily controlled the ball at full pelt and sent over exactly the piercing centre that Bennett was waiting for. His head rammed the ball into the net to leave 70,000 spectators (and several players) open-mouthed with astonishment. The victory left Arsenal (3-1 winners at Liverpool) in doubt as to who their main title challengers

The Climb to the Summit *(November 1950 – February 1951)*

were likely to be, and their visit to White Hart Lane just over a month later was already building up into a critical derby game.

A trip to Huddersfield on 25th November did not seem daunting for a Tottenham side which had now registered eight straight victories, especially since Town had failed to win in five games. But football aficionados have long grown to recognise that a stunning performance in one match is likely to be turned over in the next. And so it proved. Huddersfield hit the visitors with three rabbit punches in the first 50 minutes and it took all of Tottenham's resilience and nous to pull the scoreline round to a more respectable 2-3. The loss of both points was even more costly, because Middlesbrough and Newcastle both won to move above the Lilywhites, whilst Arsenal's fifth consecutive win kept them clear of the chasing pack. Spurs, at least, had a game in hand.

	P	W	D	L	F	A	Pts
Arsenal	19	13	4	2	45	16	30
Middlesbrough	19	11	5	3	42	22	27
Newcastle	19	10	6	3	35	26	26
SPURS	18	11	3	4	46	24	25
Manchester U	19	9	5	5	21	13	23

A glance at the League table above will confirm the significance of Spurs' home match with Middlesbrough on 2nd December. Boro had gained the reputation of being 'The Spurs of the North', because they relied more on good passing and movement than excessive dribbling and almighty hoofs. The match turned into a cracker, because both sides were going full tilt for victory and both sets of attackers had the edge over their respective defenders. After a muted opening thirteen minutes, four goals were bagged in an eight-minute spell that saw Boro twice take the lead, before being pegged back by equalisers from Ramsey (a penalty for a foul on Baily) and Duquemin. A wicked deflection off Medley put Boro back in front in the second half, but Walters saved a point in the 3-3 draw by heading in from a disputed corner. Both sets of fans were disappointed at not winning, until news filtered through of Arsenal's shock 0-3 defeat at Bolton.

A long trip north to Sheffield Wednesday, in the days when the M1 was still ten years away, was not a journey Spurs relished. Hillsborough was something of a bogey ground, with Spurs recording only one victory in 40 years. December was also a month in which Spurs traditionally wobbled. For three consecutive seasons, 1946-47 to 1948-49, Spurs were nicely poised for promotion from the Second Division before a bad run sent them spinning down the table. They had shaken off that jinx in last season's promotion run, but any slip-ups were liable to provoke a painful feeling of *déjà vu*. The other problem facing Spurs was the weather. Persistent heavy rain had left pitches across the country cutting up badly, not least at White Hart Lane, where only the wings were free of sludge. Rowe's slick-passing system was liable to literally get bogged down, some reckoned, and a heavier reliance on long balls out to the wings was the suggested solution. Rowe largely ignored these helpful tips. He knew his players were capable of maintaining possession with quick forward thrusts, whatever the underlying conditions.

Hillsborough was a mud-heap, but a 1-1 draw against the struggling Owls was due more to wayward finishing than the state of the pitch. Ramsey demonstrated this after a quarter of an hour when he sent a penalty kick soaring high into the stands. Some observers wondered if the Spurs board were going to dig deep into their pockets to buy a top-drawer centre-forward, following the example of Sunderland, who had shelled out £30,000 for Trevor Ford. As it happened, that piece of business was for the moment looking ill-judged, as Ford was firing nothing but blanks.

The main consolation to Spurs was that Arsenal were also getting jittery. They had been 3-1 up at home to Blackpool, when Stanley Matthews inspired a great comeback to put the Gunners 3-4 in arrears. A late penalty saved the home team's bacon to earn a draw, and once more there were jeers from Tottenham fans about 'Lucky Arsenal'. That tag, which has stuck to them since the 1930s, was heard again when the FA Cup draw was announced. Arsenal had a home tie against Third Division (North) Carlisle. Last season they had been given four home ties, followed by two semi-final games at White Hart Lane. The furthest they had had to travel in the Cup was the nine-mile trip to Wembley, where they had triumphed 2-0 over Liverpool. Spurs, by contrast, now faced another trip to Huddersfield, where they had just recently lost.

That FA Cup-tie was for the future. Spurs still had the small matter of a League visit to Blackpool to contend with. The Tangerines had thrashed Spurs 4-1 on the opening day, and Rowe chewed his pencil as he pondered how to blunt the deadly duo of Matthews and Mortensen. He decided to assign Bill Nicholson to provide cover for the hard-pressed left-back Willis. This would, it was hoped, quieten Matthews and cut off the main supply route for the prolific goal-getter Mortensen. In the event, an injury to Blackpool's centre-half Haylock early on, meant Spurs could afford to tie up an extra man without suffering any handicap. This enabled the rest of the players to concentrate on their passing game.

The Climb to the Summit *(November 1950 – February 1951)*

They shrugged off the atrocious wintry conditions to record a 1-0 win, courtesy of 'The Duke' who headed home a Medley cross.

Attention now switched to the big one. Arsenal had just suffered their first home defeat of the season, 0-1 against Burnley, as a result of which the Gunners had been knocked off their perch on top of the table, but were still two points ahead of fourth-placed Spurs, who had a game in hand. The match was hyped as the most-important League meeting ever between the two clubs and the interest provoked rumours that the game would be switched from White Hart Lane to Wembley, to cope with the huge crowd expected. This idea was scotched, but the headaches for the authorities were massive. The game was taking place on 23rd December, the last shopping day before Christmas. The gates were scheduled to open at 11.30am for the 2.15pm kick-off. No advance tickets were sold, despite non-stop enquiries from both sets of fans, and the ticket office at White Hart Lane was fully prepared to be besieged. Although very few people had motor cars in those days, traffic congestion was a major headache and coaches from Highbury Corner were leaving at 8.30am in order to beat the jams. Extra traffic police were on duty, some equipped with loudspeakers to redirect gridlocked traffic. Temporary signposts were erected showing alternative routes and the police urged motorists to stay clear of Tottenham High Road between noon and 5pm, though it is hard to imagine anyone being foolish enough to try it anyway. In the end, the dire warnings of chaos and locked gates frightened away the casual fans on what is traditionally always a poor day for attendances. A mere 54,893 clicked through the turnstiles to witness the much-hyped 'Clash of the Titans'.

Those fortunate enough to be inside witnessed a shift in the relative stature of the two clubs. Arsenal were outplayed by a classier team, and the Gunners' old-fashioned battering-ram tactics were made to look crude against the new-fangled Continental-style Spurs. Additionally, knowledgeable supporters on both sides were puzzled by Arsenal manager Tom Whittaker playing Freddie Cox on the left wing and McPherson on the right, when both players were happier on the opposite flanks. Although Tottenham only scraped through 1-0 (Baily nipping through a panicky defence to fire home), the score does not tell the full story, because Spurs struck the woodwork twice and created numerous other chances, whilst their rivals had only one decent scoring opportunity.

For those with a vested interest in football, Christmas Day was just another day at the office. Most Tottenham fans stayed at home with their turkey rather than make the arduous trek on public transport to Derby, but the Rams supporters turned out in large numbers and sacrificed their

Christmas pudding. They had the satisfaction of seeing their team gain a point in the 1-1 draw, though both sets of players bewailed the referee, who refused to accept that a Lee header had crossed the line for Derby, or that a Duquemin goal was legitimate for Spurs.

On Boxing Day, in line with tradition, the previous day's fixtures were reversed, so Derby visited White Hart Lane. Rowe made three changes, bringing in McClellan, Murphy and Scarth in place of Duquemin, Bennett and Walters. These were explained by injuries or fatigue (three games in four days), but were only partly successful. McClellan was a revelation, scoring both goals in the 2-1 victory, the second being particularly eye-catching as he slithered round three defenders, including the goalkeeper, before steering the ball home. Murphy was adjudged to have pulled his weight, but Scarth 'didn't fill Walter's boots', according to the report in the *Weekly Herald*.

Christmas lost all seasonal cheer for Arsenal, who stumbled to three straight defeats. After succumbing to Spurs, they were stunned by Stoke recording their season's first away win, 0-3, before being 'doubled' by the same opponents on Boxing Day. This meant the table had now taken on a different hue:

	P	W	D	L	F	A	Pts
Middlesbrough	24	14	7	3	58	31	35
SPURS	24	14	6	4	55	30	34
Wolves	24	13	5	6	51	30	31
Arsenal	25	13	5	7	49	29	31

The last fixture of 1950 saw White Hart Lane welcome a distinguished guest. Prime Minister Clement Attlee shivered in the freezing conditions along with the rest of the 54,000 crowd. The pitch was bone-hard, which seemed ideally suited to Tottenham's short-passing game. The visitors, Charlton, relied on the hefty hump up the pitch, but all too often they found their forwards didn't have time to reach the ball before it was mopped up by Tottenham's rearguard. Even so it was a close game, and Spurs had cause to thank Ramsey's positional astuteness when he cleared a ball off the goal-line with Ditchburn beaten. Spurs' goal came from Walters, who must have been practising on his ice skates, judging by the way he pirouetted and slammed the ball into the net so sharply.

Spurs clung on in the gathering gloom and midway through the second half the referee called for a white ball (instead of the usual brown one) to ease the strain on everyone's eyes. That 1-0 victory showed the clinical efficiency of Spurs and also had an added advantage. Teams level

The Climb to the Summit *(November 1950 – February 1951)*

on points were separated by goal-average (goals scored divided by goals conceded). This favoured teams with stingy defences rather than those scoring and conceding plenty. The fact that Middlesbrough could only draw meant that Spurs went top of the table, on account of a goal average 0.072 better than Boro's. It was the first time that Spurs had topped the First Division since November 1933.

	P	W	D	L	F	A	(GA)	Pts
SPURS	25	15	6	4	56	30	(1.866)	36
Middlesbrough	25	14	8	3	61	34	(1.794)	36

In those times, the FA Cup was held in higher regard by most fans than the League Championship, so the trip to Huddersfield inspired 7,000 loyal Tottenham fans to go 'Up for the Cup', where they joined 18,000 Town supporters. Those travelling from London nearly had a wasted journey. The early January weather was up to its usual tricks and the pitch was a glutinous mudbath. If that wasn't enough, thick fog had enveloped Yorkshire and the gates weren't opened until 45 minutes before kick-off when the fog lifted slightly.

Spurs outplayed Huddersfield, but it wasn't enough. The Terriers lived up to their nickname by snapping at the ankles of the Spurs players, and in one instance actually felled a Lilywhite by grabbing hold of his lower leg. Tottenham shrugged off these roughhouse tactics and concentrated on their football, but with the forwards shooting inaccurately it was of little benefit. The other problem was that the mud and puddles meant players often waited for passes that got stuck.

The second half carried on in similar vein, but towards the end Spurs' players collectively lost patience with Town's endless fouling and decided to 'mix it'. This loss of composure seemed to play into the home side's hands, for they struck quickly with two decisive goals. Arthur Rowe summed up the game by stating that: 'Our lads were provoked by considerable spoiling tactics, but had they maintained their equanimity and got on with the football, as in the first half, the result would have been much different.' One can only speculate what language a manager nowadays would have used under similar circumstances.

Though the FA Cup defeat was galling for Tottenham supporters, the insignificance of the outcome was brought into focus when news came through that a coach carrying Spurs fans had collided with a lorry and that two teenage boys – Albert Wood and James Dent – had lost their lives. Representatives of the club, the players and the supporters attended the funerals. Amongst the wreaths was one from Charlton Athletic

Supporters Club, whilst those from the Spurs players and the club appropriately consisted of white lilies and lilies of the valley.

In time-honoured fashion that 0-2 Cup defeat led everyone at Spurs to 'concentrate on the League'. They had to, because the next game was at Old Trafford against Manchester United, who although uncharacteristically hovering just above halfway, were still regarded as one of the top sides, and so they proved. Although Spurs took the lead through Baily, the Red Devils fought back and by early in the second half Jack Rowley had put United into a 2-1 lead. Though Tottenham threw everything they could at them, they couldn't break through and in the end were reliant on Ditchburn to keep the score down whenever United broke quickly from defence to attack. Poor Ted injured his shoulder blade in the process, and Willis was also a casualty with a crocked knee. Paradoxically, Spurs actually increased their lead at the top to 0.106 on goal average, because Middlesbrough lost 1-3 at Arsenal.

Tottenham's Supporters Club were a thoughtful bunch of people, highlighted by the way they had formed a 'Willie Hall Trust Fund' to assist their favourite player of the 1930s. Hall, a short, chubby player had made over 200 appearances for Spurs and made history when he scored five goals in 28 minutes whilst playing against Northern Ireland in 1938. Sadly, Hall had succumbed to a disease that had necessitated both legs being amputated. His condition required several operations and the trust fund was a godsend to him. The Supporters Club also funded a gramophone, so that the Spurs team could entertain themselves on long trips away with what would now be called impromptu karaoke sessions.

Spurs faced another tough test in their championship bid with the visit of Wolves – the form team of the moment, unbeaten since 11th November. Both teams struggled in the cloying White Hart Lane mud, especially the defences, which failed to keep tabs on the livelier forwards. Billy Wright had been the mainstay right-half for England for four seasons, and the Spurs No 4, Bill Nicholson, found it impossible to dislodge the incumbent. Any England selectors watching, however, would have witnessed Wright suffer a shocker. He failed to contain Walters and Murphy, who harried him relentlessly. Unfortunately, it didn't do Nicholson any favours, because he too suffered an off-day. Also displaying loss of form was Eddie Baily – the 'Cheeky Chappie' – who had been burning himself out on the heavy grounds during Britain's wettest winter of recent times.

Murphy was the man of the match. He turned up all over the pitch, surging forward to create attacks, and then rushing back to aid the defence from wolfish breakaways. It was Murphy's endeavours that led to the Hotspur's opening goal, scored by McClellan. Walters added the second to put the game beyond the reach of Wolves, who only managed to pull one goal back, despite probably deserving at least a point for their efforts.

That 2-1 victory proved to be an opportune time for Arthur Rowe to assess the way the season was panning out: 'I estimated in advance that we would be lying third at the New Year, but we came out on top, and there I think we shall stay.' This tentative prediction was encouraged by casting his eyes over the fixture list for the rest of the season and spotting that eleven of the remaining fifteen fixtures were against teams in the lower half of the table.

	P	W	D	L	F	A	Pts
SPURS	27	16	6	5	59	33	38
Middlesbrough	27	15	8	4	64	38	38
Arsenal	28	15	6	7	56	32	36
Newcastle	26	13	7	6	46	38	33

Tottenham's early Cup exit meant they had no fixture on 27th January, so they travelled to Ninian Park for a friendly with Second Division Cardiff City. This enabled Rowe to experiment by bringing in Garwood to replace the flu-ridden Nicholson, and Adams, who took Medley's place. Both acquitted themselves well, though not well enough to usurp the senior players from the team. For Adams the game was especially memorable, as he volleyed in a goal in the 3-2 victory in front of 11,000. The fact that it was a friendly also enabled the Bluebirds to make two substitutions when their goalkeeper and centre-half concussed themselves in a heavy collision.

The next League game produced another intriguing clash, for it sent Spurs up to the 'Millionaire's Club', namely Sunderland. Since their last meeting in September, the Rokerites' boss Bill Murray had splashed out £30,000 on striker Trevor Ford, and obtained a couple of defenders to shore up a porous defence. Sunderland were widely perceived as wanting to buy their way to success. It wasn't working, judging by the table, because they were plodding along in the bottom half, though they were generally regarded as an improving side.

Harry Clarke was detailed to man-mark Ford, and did so with aplomb, neutralising the threat from the under-performing star. Sunderland's new-look defence operated efficiently and both sets of forwards were off colour. The goalless draw marked the first occasion this season that Tottenham had failed to score, which is remarkable considering just how much flak had been directed at the attack. The rude fact shows that in 28 League games Spurs had scored 59 goals, an average of over two per game. No side since the War had exceeded two goals per game in capturing the title. More likely, the criticism stemmed from the fact that the forwards weren't converting a higher percentage of the chances that the playmakers creating. It is reasonable to surmise that had the forwards been more clinical, then the team might have been aiming towards a century of League goals, instead of the more likely 90. That magic century hadn't been achieved by any First Division club since Manchester City in 1936-37.

Curiously, Tottenham's defence had attracted considerable praise, but if anything, they were shipping a higher quota of goals than had been the case of recent championship sides. Spurs had conceded 33 goals in those 28 games so far, well in excess of a goal a game. None of the previous three title-winners had exceeded a goal per game, though both Arsenal and Portsmouth (twice) were noted for their mean defences. In reality, there was little cause for concern at either end of the pitch for Tottenham, as long as they stayed ahead of the pack. Despite drawing with Sunderland, they extended their lead at the top to a full point, on account of Middlesbrough losing.

Spurs played a friendly at Standard Liege in Belgium on Tuesday, 6th February, winning 4-1. This allowed them the weekend off, as it was set aside for the FA Cup fifth round. Half the first team travelled to see Spurs' reserves lose 1-2 at home to Brentford's in the Combination Cup, though Duquemin and Bennett were required to play. Indeed, it was the Duke who supplied Bennett with the chip that led to Tottenham's goal. There was better news for the 'A' team, which won 5-1 against Ipswich reserves in a 'home' game at Hoddesdon. Occasional first-teamers Scarth and Uphill were in that side. Undoubtedly Spurs fans were even happier at learning that Arsenal had been dumped out of the FA Cup 0-1 at Manchester United

The enforced break gave 'Fanfare', the feature writer in the *Weekly Herald*, the chance to spark a debate on the lot of the average supporter. He was unhappy that Birmingham City proposed to increase admission prices from one shilling (5p) to one shilling and threepence (over 6p). He felt that too little was being spent on the grounds to justify any increase and pointed out that few stadia had as much as two-thirds covered accommodation in the same way that White Hart Lane did (50,000 out of 75,000). He argued that it was time for transfer fees to be reduced; more money should be spent on youth teams, and more money on the grounds. Only then could clubs justify charging the supporters more for watching

The Climb to the Summit *(November 1950 – February 1951)*

their football. He even advocated all-seater stadia, long before these became a reality at Aberdeen and Coventry City.

The following Saturday it was business as usual, with first-team football returning to the Lane. The visitors, Aston Villa, were another side whose chairman had flashed his chequebook, though they were more fearful of dropping through the relegation trapdoor. He had spent £62,000 on four players – a phenomenal sum for the time. Spurs probably hadn't spent that much on transfer purchases in their history.

Another pre-match deluge required another bout of frantic fork-stabbing by the groundsmen as they sought to drain the standing water from the pitch, though they could do nothing about the cloying, ankle-deep mud which had replaced the once-lush grass. Chief groundsman Henry Naylor was frustrated by a combination of compacted turf and damaged drainage that didn't allow the water to escape. The White Hart Lane pitch featured a pronounced crown in the middle, due to twenty years of excessive sanding, which under normal circumstances helped to steer the water away from harm's way, but the incessant rain had literally swamped the ground. The inclement weather also contributed to a stay-away by fans and the attendance dropped to 47,842, the lowest figure since August.

It was a pity, because they missed an eventful and controversial match. It didn't seem to be heading that way, as Spurs seized a first-half lead through Baily, who decided the best way to avoid the mud was to have a crack from 25 yards. When Medley made it 2-0 a minute into the second half, it appeared to be all over, but Villa struck twice to equalise and cause hearts to flutter. Although the loss of Bill Nicholson with a leg injury (his first absence of the season) may partly explain the trouble, it is somewhat unfair, because Cliff Brittan was an admirable replacement. Once again it was the forwards who failed to stick away enough of their chances, though in fairness Joe Rutherford played well in the visitors' goal.

Then, ten minutes before the end, came the main talking point. Ramsey had ventured forward in a daring foray into the opposition box and had been duly brought down by a careless tackle. No problem there, it was a clear penalty. There then followed an amusing game of 'find the penalty spot in the mud', which was eventually won by the referee. Ramsey strode up and struck the penalty well, but Rutherford continued his hot form by blocking it. The lineman flagged to indicate Rutherford had illegally moved, and despite Villa protests, the referee ordered a retake. Ramsey made no mistake this time, and his kick earned a 3-2 victory to replicate that earned at Villa Park in September. Many spectators must have suspected that Tottenham were fielding Lady Luck as an extra player, especially the opposition supporters who watched their side slip to next-to-bottom. With West Brom earning a 2-0 win over Arsenal, the margin between the north London sides widened to four points.

A visit to Turf Moor was next on the cards, and Burnley's tight defence would once again provide a stiff challenge for the much-maligned Tottenham forwards. As it happened, the clamour for change up front now reached a crescendo as once again they under-performed. The persuasive Arthur Rowe had talked Alex Wright out of his transfer request; no doubt telling him his time would come. Len Duquemin had put in a compelling case by netting a hat-trick for the reserves from the inside-left position. To make matters worse for Rowe, luck deserted his team, and twice the Spurs' defence protested in vain at awarded goals. Ditchburn claimed he'd been impeded for the first, whilst Clarke insisted his handball for the penalty was accidental. Both Burnley goals were dispatched by outside-right Chew, which led to a myriad of puns from the various newspaper reporters. You shall be spared them, dear reader.

Defeat did not prove too costly as Middlesbrough didn't play, and Arsenal were trounced 2-5 by Charlton at Highbury. Both sets of rival north London supporters put aside their natural enmity for a better cause, organising a darts match to swell the coffers of a trust fund for the families of the two young Spurs fans killed in the coach crash. The fund had been started by the Supporters Club and been boosted by a fifty-guinea (£52.50) donation from the Tottenham directors. The fund eventually reached £500 by the end of the season.

Chapter 4

~ THE MARCH TO THE TITLE ~

(March-May 1951)

In the wake of the defeat at Burnley, it was Alex Wright who won the tussle with the Duke for the right to replace the beleaguered McClellan at No 9, and Wright spectacularly rewarded his manager's faith by scoring within five minutes of his debut, at home to Chelsea. Baily created the second goal by dancing through the Pensioners' defence to set up Burgess, whereupon the whole Spurs side switched to auto-pilot and sleepwalked through the second half against a wretched Chelsea side who were just off the foot of the table. The visitors pulled a goal back, but even that couldn't shake Spurs out of their slumbers. It got so bad that a pigeon was able to perch safely on top of the Chelsea goal without fearing for his life from a Lilywhite shot. The other talking point came when Mr R Burgess (the Spurs player) was brought down in the penalty area and Mr R Burgess (the referee) failed to award a penalty. This prompted chanting throughout the ground that brought blushes to any visiting ladies and anger to any member of the referee's immediate family (assuming they weren't Spurs fans).

Once again, the other results went Spurs' way. Middlesbrough lost and Arsenal's 1-3 defeat at Old Trafford effectively ended the Gunners' title bid. Newcastle were the dark horses sneaking up on the rails, still harbouring hopes of a League and Cup double, which had eluded every team since 1897. Following Spurs win over Chelsea, the state of play on the evening of 3rd March 1951 was:

	P	W	D	L	F	A	Pts
SPURS	31	18	7	6	64	38	43
Middlesbrough	30	16	8	6	68	43	40
Manchester U	31	16	6	9	47	33	38
Newcastle	29	15	8	6	50	39	38

News of the emergence of Tottenham Hotspur as a footballing force had spread far beyond England's shores, to a world that retained it's fascination with English football. The Argentinian FA offered Spurs £12,000 to undertake a six-match tour of the South American country, whilst Le Havre FC made a more modest, but perhaps more realistic offer of £1,000 to tempt Spurs to a challenge match in France. The Spurs board remained tight-lipped about their summer plans, apart from the already-announced international 'Festival of Britain' tournament.

But Arthur Rowe's thoughts were concentrated solely in England's green and pleasant waterlogged land, more precisely on the Victoria Ground in Stoke, where Tottenham's championship-seekers were currently appearing. Poor Arthur was laid low with illness, so his imagination must have been running riot as he lay on his sickbed as kick-off time approached. He would have felt far worse had he been present to watch the shambles unfolding in the Potteries. Stoke were a mediocre side that should have succumbed readily to the invention and flair of the white and blues, but somebody different was writing this episode. Alex Wright, who had for so long clamoured to be in the side, fluffed his chances to make a claim for permanent establishment, most notably when he was put through by Murphy, only to watch in horror as his shot sliced wildly off his old leather boot. The Spurs defence was still initiating a steady wave of attacks, which the midfield was able to convert into goalscoring opportunities, but yet again the few visiting fans who had travelled north were left to kick the hoardings in frustration as chance after chance went begging. Fortunately, Stoke's principal striker, Mullard, was having no more luck with his aim and the match fizzled out into a goalless stalemate. The result left those supporters who had turned up at White Hart Lane to watch the reserves lose 1-2 to Chelsea's just as disappointed, when the scoreboards paraded around the ground every fifteen minutes resolutely refused to change. The gloom was partially lightened when news spread on the grapevine that Middlesbrough had dropped a point at home, thereby maintaining the three-point gap at the top.

As supporters assembled that evening in the various hostelries around north London, the main topic of conversation was the stuttering forward line that had only managed five goals in five games. The considered view was that Duquemin should be restored to the first-team forthwith, though his many admirers weren't helped by the fact that he had played poorly for the reserves. The other change that would have proved popular was the restoration of Les Bennett. The inside-right had just got married and there were rumours flying around that Aston Villa were interested in luring the newly-weds away from one smoky city to another..

Arthur Rowe appreciated that the championship challenge was being eroded by these underwhelming performances, so for the 17th March game at home to West Brom he restored Bennett and Duquemin to the team, dropping Medley and Wright to make way for them. Only 45,000 gathered inside White Hart Lane, but they made up for their lack of numbers by creating a wall of noise that built up inside the ground as the game progressed and spilled over into the surrounding streets. The first eruption of sound came when the teams ran onto the pitch and the team-changes became apparent. The second volley of cheers exploded when Nicholson guided the ball into the path of the Duke, who smashed the ball home. West Brom weathered the encroaching storm, throwing bodies around to prevent certain goals and leaving goalkeeper Jim Sanders caked in mud.

Though the game was theoretically still up for grabs at 1-0, the half-time chatter was more relaxed and confident than usual, and the players in the home dressing room must have been scratching at the door like dogs on heat in order to start the second half. Inevitably, the striped wall of plucky Baggies began to crumble as Spurs battered against it. Bennett beat three men, sent Walters galloping down the right, and Duquemin headed his cross in. That signalled the dam-burst, and three more goals came quickly. The Duke earned his first hat-trick of the season by converting a Murphy cross, then turned provider as Bennett got his just reward. Murphy created the fifth goal by racing almost the full length of the pitch and laying the ball off to Baily. The 5-0 rout restored the belief amongst everybody at the club in the eventual destination of the title, especially when it emerged that Middlesbrough had succumbed against Fulham to extend the gap to five points. A good Easter campaign would surely leave the others too far behind to realistically catch the rampant Lilywhites.

Three games in four days is hard work for players more used to playing once a week, and after an unchanged side had ground out a 1-0 win at Fulham on Good Friday, Rowe rested Bennett for the following day's trip to Portsmouth and gave Dennis Uphill his second game of the season. Pompey did not need telling that they had effectively relinquished the title they had held for two seasons, but they made Spurs work hard for the 1-1 draw, as if to make them prove that they were worthy successors. Though Pompey took an early lead, the resurgent Uphill levelled by positioning himself on the end of a Burgess free-kick. Easter Monday's return fixture with Fulham at the Lane saw a rejuvenated Bennett score the opening goal, though the forward line started misfiring before the end of the match. Thankfully it had been won by that time.

Curiously, the Easter sequence of scores (1-0, 1-1, 2-1) duplicated those achieved during the Christmas holiday period. The first of the Easter games (at Fulham) was mostly spoiled for those travelling Spurs' fans who turned up at Craven Cottage half an hour before kick-off, for they discovered that demand for space on the terraces far exceeded the supply. By the time the diehards had barged their way into the ground, half-time was only ten minutes away. Many others, having already parted with their 'one and threepence' (6p), gave up long before this and made their way back home in the pouring rain.

Spurs were now four points clear of the pack with just six games to go. The most likely threat to their supremacy was now posed by perennial bridesmaids Manchester United, who had won ten out of their last eleven games. Not only were they the form team, but they also had what on paper looked the easier run-in, giving hope that they could whittle down the Londoners' four-point advantage. Two points adrift of Matt Busby's team were Middlesbrough, whose form had faded, but they enjoyed a game in hand on the two clubs above them. The fourth and fifth placed teams were virtually out of it, but still lurking in sixth place were the dark (stripy) horses known as Newcastle United. Although ten points behind Spurs, their magnificent Cup run had produced a backlog of fixtures which meant they had an extra three League games to squeeze in. Even if they won them all, they would still be four points behind, and the fact that they faced a 'four-pointer' at home to Manchester United a week before the Cup final was reckoned to be a further hindrance, as undoubtedly the final against Blackpool would take precedence in manager Stan Seymour's eyes.

Arthur Rowe was confident that his lads would ultimately prevail. According to his meticulous forecasting, Spurs should have been level with the leaders after Easter, relying on a run-in with four home games out of six to carry them to their first title. He was delighted with the four-point cushion, which was a blessed relief because, as the hackneyed cliché goes, the mud is a great leveller, and nowhere was there more mud than at White Hart Lane.

The first game of the run-in was reckoned to be a home banker against relegation-haunted Everton. It appeared that Tottenham thought so too, because they sleepwalked their way through the first half, relying on Everton being too witless to score. That theory misfired when the Toffeemen put the ball into the net just after the turnaround, only for a flagging linesman to deny them their just desserts. Spurs woke up after that, and the tension was released when three goals were scored without reply. The middle goal came straight from the training ground. Dead-ball specialist Ramsey floated a free-kick over the defence and Murphy stole in behind to head home. It was a standard set-piece for Tottenham. Murphy's joy at scoring would have been tempered by the report he read in the local paper that blamed his persistent hesitancy for holding up many of Spurs' moves, and that he could not, in all seriousness, contest Medley's place.

Harry Clarke had escaped criticism, as a member of the defence that had shorn up the title challenge. Along with goalie Ditchburn, Clarke was the only ever-present in the side. He got married this week, and unsurprisingly in the circumstances spurned a traditional Saturday wedding in favour of a Monday do.

Although Rowe was no doubt concerned about burning his players out, he magnanimously agreed to provide a trio of first-teamers to star in a benefit game for the former Leyton Orient player Ledger Ritson, who had recently had a leg amputated.

The penultimate away match of the season was a trip to Newcastle. The Geordies were still smarting from the 7-0 annihilation meted out to them in November, but were naturally distracted by the seasonal showcase of the FA Cup final. This meant that they had only picked up two points from their last three games, and their outside chance of capturing the League title had slowly dissolved. Their main goal-threat to Spurs came from the incomparable JET Milburn, whose initials were especially apt. With an aversion to heading the leather cannonballs that passed for footballs, Milburn relied on speed and strength to spreadeagle defences and sharpshooting to finish the job off. Harry Clarke was detailed to man-mark him, and it's doubtful whether his new wife had spent as much time in close proximity to him as 'Wor Jackie' did that afternoon.

With Newcastle's attack castrated, it was up to Spurs to inflict damage at the other end. They achieved this after seven minutes with the sucker punch of that well-worked free-kick routine that had hoodwinked defences up and down the land. Obviously it was a novelty to the men in striped shirts because they stood stock still as Willis floated the kick far beyond them to where Sonny Walters stole in to dispatch it. It was perhaps just as well that the visitors struck so early, because an injury to Bennett forced him to become a spectator on the left wing, which naturally blunted the Tottenham knife. The Tynesiders plugged away remorselessly, but were unable to penetrate the back line, which once again held sway. In their last ten away games, Spurs had only conceded two goals on two occasions, and this time they posted another clean sheet – Ditchburn's fifth in the last seven games. The push and run system was able to function at its most efficient on a peach of a pitch, though it had also coped admirably with the ploughed fields that passed for playing surfaces elsewhere, not least their own at White Hart Lane.

The 1-0 victory at Newcastle almost certainly ensured that the title was bound for Tottenham for the first time. Manchester United had lost, and the gap between first and second was now a yawning six points with only four games to go. Additionally, Tottenham had a far superior goal-average, due to having scored 77 goals – fifteen more than the Red Devils. The Mancunians' boast of being the best club in Lancashire was even under threat as a resurgent Blackpool had stormed into third place, elbowing aside Middlesbrough. They, too, were effectively an extra point behind Spurs, because their defence had conceded 47 goals, seven more than Ditchburn had let in. All the Lilywhites had to do was win one of their remaining games, or even draw a couple, to guarantee the trophy was theirs. Even four defeats wouldn't matter, as long as Manchester United lost a game, which was highly probable since they had yet to play Newcastle and Blackpool – the two Cup finalists. It was now more a question of where, not if.

	P	W	D	L	F	A	Pts
SPURS	38	23	9	6	77	40	55
Manchester U	38	21	7	10	62	39	49
Blackpool	38	19	9	10	75	47	47
Middlesbrough	37	18	10	9	73	56	46

There were 55,000 inside White Hart Lane on 14th April, enjoying the usual marched band entertainment before the kick-off. They hoped they were in the right place to see the new kings of soccer crowned. There was just one teeny problem. Their opponents were Huddersfield, who had already inflicted two defeats on the would-be champions. Despite being embroiled in the relegation scrap at the bottom of the table, they seemed to have fathomed a way of dealing with all this fancy pushing and running, and they duly claimed their third Tottenham scalp in one season. The 0-2 defeat was Spurs' first loss on their own ground since Blackpool had whipped them on the opening day.

How had lightning struck for a third time? What was Huddersfield's secret weapon? Nothing in particular. The Tottenham attack suffered another attack of the collywobbles, which seemed to strike them randomly, and wayward finishing helped the worst defence in the division look impenetrable. Goalkeeper Wheeler impressed with a marvellous acrobatic display to deny any efforts that were on target, and the Yorkshire team's forwards were able to teach Spurs a thing or two with goals either side of the interval. Spurs fans may have attempted to use the absence of right-back Ramsey as an excuse, but the Terriers likewise had a player missing, playing for England against the Scots in the Home International Championship. Though Harry Hassall didn't gain a win on his international debut, he at least had the consolation of scoring the first England goal in the 2-3 defeat.

Spurs' defeat was just one of those things, perhaps, but Huddersfield did resort to one underhand tactic. That Tottenham free-kick routine was attempted once too often. Metcalfe spotted Walters about to run in on the blind side and simply stood in front of him to obstruct him. Naughty, but undoubtedly effective.

Manchester United and Blackpool both won their games to keep up the pressure, but Middlesbrough lost. The Blackpool win was especially remarkable because they achieved it without their spearhead, Matthews and Mortensen, who were also at Wembley. Now the pundits were practising their long division in a bid to calculate what Manchester United had to do to overcome their inferior goal-average. They calculated that if United won all their games 1-0 and Spurs won one game 1-0 and lost the others 0-2, then Busby's team would prevail. It was all a theoretical exercise, of little practical use, but it made the less confident Spurs' fans just a little jittery. The reserve side, too, were experiencing some problems at the top of the Combination Cup table, because they had just lost to Arsenal's second string 0-2 at Highbury on the Monday.

Tottenham's next opportunity to put the championship to bed came with a trip up to Middlesbrough. Although their opponents' title ambitions had quietly faded, this was far from an easy fixture. Despite the absence of maestro Wilf Mannion, the Boro were able to string together a succession of attacks to keep the Spurs defence on tenterhooks. Mannion's replacement, Fitzsimmons, squandered the best of these by panicking and firing wide when clean through against Ditchburn. Murphy had better luck with his finishing. Attempting a speculative lob from 30 yards he watched in a combination of ecstasy and disbelief as the ball sailed over Ugolini's head and fell into the net.

If Middlesbrough fans felt hard done by, they were soon appeased. Walker had been leading Ramsey a merry dance down the left wing, and now he did so again and crossed for Spuhler's equaliser. Tottenham were fortunate to keep the score at 1-1 for the rest of the match and escape with a valuable, yet inconclusive point. Elsewhere, Blackpool had lost, terminating their previously slim chance, but Manchester United won, leaving them three points behind with only two games left.

Arthur Rowe would doubtless have preferred to take his team back to London to prepare for next Saturday's crucial encounter with Sheffield Wednesday, but a long-arranged friendly had been inserted into the fixture list. Doubtless it had made perfect sense at the time for Spurs to head north to Edinburgh, when they were already halfway up there, but with the benefit of hindsight it was an unwelcome distraction. The Monday encounter with runaway Scottish champions Hibernian could have been billed as a British Championship game, but it wasn't taken too seriously and both teams concentrated on giving an entertaining exhibition, which they did, despite the 0-0 scoreline. The other game taking place that day was the concluding fixture of the Football Combination. Tottenham reserves' hopes of landing that trophy were dashed when Arsenal reserves cruised to a 3-0 win at White Hart Lane.

Two home games now remained for the first team to wrap things up. The first of these, against Sheffield Wednesday on 28th April, was packed with significance. On the final day of the previous season, Wednesday had clinched promotion by drawing 0-0 at Hillsborough against the champions, Spurs. This season saw the two promoted clubs at opposite ends of the table, and the desperate Owls had shed out a British record transfer fee to Notts County for inside-right Jackie Sewell. Another oddity was that Spurs hadn't won any of their six games against Yorkshire opponents all season, with Huddersfield claiming three victories, and Wednesday and Middlesbrough (twice) earning draws. For those readers who are too young, Middlesbrough was indeed part of Yorkshire before the Government started mucking around with the various county boundaries in the 1970s.

Tottenham fielded the same line-up as they had at Middlesbrough, which meant that there was no place for Bennett, much to the annoyance of his many fans who pointed out that the club's more anxious performances tended to coincide with his absence. He was being kept out by Medley, who had recovered from a stomach injury, but Murphy had switched across the pitch to Bennett's position, because Murphy had been wearing Medley's No 11 shirt.

Arthur Rowe also figured that Spurs had reached the top on a quagmire of a home pitch, so now the rainy season had ended, he ordered the groundsmen to soak it. The greasy surface certainly aided the intricate passing and off-the-ball movement that had been the talking point of football all that season. The ball zigzagged its way up the field whilst a plethora of white shirts jinked and darted past the bemused Wednesday players. It was a display worthy of any team who proclaimed themselves the best in the land, apart from one fault that had dogged them all season. They still converted too few of the chances created. Against Wednesday, Murphy was the chief culprit. Why he was off form is a matter of conjecture. Was it just an off-day that every footballer suffers from? Or was the tension of the occasion playing on his mind? Either way he appeared to be in two minds when presented with a goalscoring

The March to the Title (March-May 1951)

chance, whether to shoot or pass to a better-placed colleague. Invariably he chose the wrong option. It was an affliction that seemed to have struck most of the Spurs forwards at intervals during the season and it caused headaches for Arthur Rowe. Mercifully, the build up was remorseless. Even if the forwards were only tucking away one chance in ten, it still meant that victory was more likely than not.

As described in the introduction to this book, the game ended with Tottenham Hotspur the new champions of the Football League, because Manchester United could no longer catch them.

	P	W	D	L	F	A	Pts
SPURS	41	24	10	7	79	43	58
Manchester U	41	24	7	10	73	39	55

There was still one game to play, and the fixture list had with foresight decreed that Liverpool would be the visitors. One wonders if the two teams had colluded to put on an exhibition for the distinguished group of spectators, who included members of the Argentinian squad who were due to face England the following week, and FC Austria who were playing Spurs on the Monday. Though Liverpool were only a mid-table side, they played their part in a competitive, enthralling game that was a wonderful advertisement for English football. Tottenham won the match 3-1, which took them up to a grand total of 60 points for a 42-match season, the first club to achieve that landmark since Arsenal twenty years previously.

After the game, the majority of the near-50,000 crowd leapt over the barriers and encircled the space in front of the directors box to hear Arthur Drewry, President of the Football League, officially present the coveted trophy to skipper Ron Burgess. Mr Drewry pronounced that the rest of the League's clubs were proud of Spurs, not only for winning the trophy, but also for the way they had done it. He also shouted out to the assembled throng: 'What are you going to do in 1952?' The answer mirrored the supporters' preoccupation with what they regarded as an even more precious piece of silverware: 'Win the Cup!' The fans then turned their attention to the architect of their team's success by chanting: 'We want Arthur,' until the great man stepped forward to deliver his own judgment. 'It's a great truth that you try things once and if you like them you try them again. That is what we are hoping to do in the future.'

Though the fans weren't naturally inclined to pay too much attention to the bottom of the table, they may have been a trifle sad that their fellow promotion side of last season, Sheffield Wednesday, fell victim on the final day. Everton, Wednesday and Chelsea had all finished with 32 points and an identical record of twelve wins and eight draws, but Chelsea earned a reprieve by not conceding as many goals as the other two and escaped the trapdoor.

Tottenham's season wasn't over yet. Two days after the culmination of the League campaign, the Festival of Britain football celebration began. The same eleven which had played against Liverpool, with the exception of Withers who replaced Ramsey, wearily took the field in front of 30,000 at the Lane to play FC Austria. The Austrians put on a display all of their own. They had taken push and run a couple of notches further, and seemingly operated a set of rules that forbade anything more than a ten-yard pass. In their natty mauve shirts, they confused the English champions by beating them at their own game. Deservedly they won the game 1-0 through a thrilling goal by Ocvirk, who had received a defence-splitting pass and swivelled to beat Ditchburn. After the shock of last-season's World Cup finals, this was another reminder to insular British footballers, that they weren't the masters of the game they had once imagined they were.

A happier occasion for all came on the Wednesday, when Tottenham's players attended a 'Grand Celebration Dance' at the lively 'Royal' on Tottenham High Road. Four and a half hours of dancing to Ivor Kirchin and his Ballroom Orchestra was on offer for a sum of 10s 6d (52½p). Then it was back to the second Festival of Britain match, at home to West Germany's Borussia Dortmund on 12th May, which gave Arthur Rowe the chance to field a more experimental line-up, featuring Brittan and McClellan, neither of whom had made a minimum fourteen League appearances required in order to earn a championship medal. Also making his first appearance was Tony Marchi, who replaced Burgess and thus became the only Tottenham player to play in the first teams in both of their championship-winning sides ten years apart.

The Germans played a similar style to the Austrians, and if some old-timers were to be believed, both Continental sides had modelled their play on the Tottenham team of the 1920s, though that sounds like wishful thinking. The English champions strode into a two-goal lead through Murphy's opportunism and Baily's long-distance shooting prowess. An injury to Ditchburn saw him leave the field with a fractured finger, at which point the 29,000 crowd witnessed the novelty of a substitution – a new-fangled idea which wouldn't reach the Football League until 1965. Onto the pitch trotted Charlie Withers, who was more used to replacing left-back Willis. Withers stood just 5ft 6½in, over six inches shorter than Ditchburn, but he proved himself a more-than-capable goalkeeper. He denied the Germans for 45 minutes, apart from a long-range effort that proved the value of Ditchburn's extra reach.

Bill Nicholson also achieved the accolade of playing for England against Portugal on 19th May. He certainly made an impact, scoring after nineteen seconds, which remains the fastest-ever debut goal by an England player. A fat lot of good it did him. Billy Wright was so dominant in that position that Nicholson never won another England cap.

After the protracted Festival of Britain, the triumphant Spurs players were still unable to relax. They nipped off to Paris to play Racing Club (winning 4-2), and at the end of May undertook a mini-tour of Denmark, taking on three Danish representative outfits and posting handsome results of 4-2, 2-2 and 2-0. Not until the beginning of June could Tottenham Hotspur's heroes put their feet up and bask in the glory of being Champions of England.

Chapter 5

~ THE TEN-YEAR ITCH ~
(1951-60)

Tottenham fans hoped the club could build on the foundations of their Championship and go on to dominate the 1950s as rivals Arsenal had dominated the 1930s. Early-season results in 1951-52 were pretty good, with six wins in the opening ten matches – an improvement over the title-winning season. The best of these wins was a 6-1 hiding of Stoke City at the Victoria Ground on 15th September, though two weeks earlier Spurs had had to eat some humble pie of their own. A resurgent Newcastle, desperate to avenge the previous season's 0-7 mauling at the Lane, belted the ball past Ditchburn seven times. Tottenham's only consolation was bagging a couple of token goals for themselves.

By mid-November, Tottenham were nicely placed, but then the rains came. White Hart Lane's badly-compacted pitch was still unable to withstand repeated inundations. Though many fans and pundits cite the pitch as the reason why Tottenham faded away badly that winter, pointing out that better February weather brought a corresponding improvement in results, it only paints half a picture. Tottenham had performed imperiously on heavy pitches the season before. Nor was their form noticeably better on good away pitches in December and January – in fact they notched only one away win in seven attempts. One of these defeats was 0-2 at Old Trafford, which handed the initiative to Manchester United. Busby's team went on to claim the title by a four-point margin from Spurs, whose thirteen-match unbeaten end to the season came too late to affect the outcome. Paradoxically, Tottenham were grateful to the Red Devils for thrashing Arsenal in their last game 6-1, thus simultaneously denying the Gunners the title, and allowing Spurs to creep above them on goal-average.

Rowe kept faith with his core players throughout the next few seasons, and though this loyalty was understandable, perhaps it may be said that he failed to inject new blood quickly enough. His innovative push and run tactics were not so suited to older legs as to young ones. The burden of all that running started to tell, and the reserves who sometimes came in were merely adequate. Even little inside-forward Tommy Harmer was used sparingly until the Rowe era was over.

The other factor that hampered the team was that by now everyone knew what to expect from Tottenham's tactics. Footballers and managers in those days were accustomed to most teams playing in the conventional way, and they were at first perplexed when confronted with something alien to them. Gradually the novelty wore off, and the more astute, free-thinking opponents were able to find ways to counteract Tottenham's system. Opposition players started to predict the off-the-ball runs of the white-shirted players and blocked the space they needed. Defenders aped the Tottenham tactic of withdrawing *en masse* whenever danger threatened, denying the attackers any space in which to operate. Revolutionary tactics tend to work, if they work at all, for about six to twelve months, depending on the level of sophistication. Tottenham had extended push and run's shelf life to two seasons because they switched divisions in the middle. In order to keep the momentum going, Rowe needed to inject new ideas into the plan to keep it fresh, or alternatively, compromise its purity. He was partly successful. Tottenham remained in the public's consciousness as one of the top clubs, a status they had never enjoyed before, but the results worsened year by year and the team slipped ever downwards. Tottenham finished mid-table in 1952-53, but it was the FA Cup campaign that dominated the fans' thoughts that year.

Irrespective of the League Championship, the FA Cup still retained its position as the premier competition, strange as that might sound to younger readers. There was no other way for a club to reach Wembley in those days, and in the absence of distractions like Europe and the League Cup, it provided the only opportunity of glory if a team was out of the running for the championship by January. It had been over 30 years since Tottenham's last FA Cup triumph, and the new generation of fans were getting restless, especially since the last success was in the days before Wembley. In other words, the only current Tottenham players to have sampled the national stadium's hallowed turf were those who pulled on England's white jerseys.

The FA Cup trail in 1952-53 had not been comfortable. A 1-1 draw at Tranmere might easily have ended in defeat, even though Spurs asserted themselves in the replay against their Third Division (North) opponents to the tune of 9-1. Another away draw against a Lancashire side followed in round four, though Preston proved much tougher opponents in the replay, as they only missed out on the League Championship that season on goal-average behind Arsenal. Tottenham scraped through 1-0, then overcame a Halifax team appearing in the fifth round for only the second time in their history. Tottenham won 3-0 at the Shay. The quarter-finals proved to be a marathon affair against Second Division Birmingham City.

After two draws, it needed a second replay, at Molineux, and Tottenham crept into the semi-finals with a 1-0 win.

By this stage, many Spurs supporters were convinced their team were destined to win the Cup, though optimistic fans of the other three semi-finalists no doubt felt the same, whether their progress had been tortuous or easy. Blackpool were the only obstacle standing between Spurs and Wembley, and the match was billed in north London as the chance to avenge the 1948 defeat at the same stage by the same club. Even the Villa Park setting was the same.

The match was perfectly balanced at 1-1 as it headed towards extra-time. Then came a moment of despair for one of Tottenham's finest players. Alf Ramsey played a routine back-pass – as was permitted in those days – to Ted Ditchburn, only to realise in horror that he'd under-hit it. Blackpool's Jackie Mudie was lurking with intent and pounced to win the game for the Tangerines. Tottenham players were distraught. Ramsey looked to shift some of the blame, pointing out that others had played their part by not being in their correct positions to receive his pass. But his criticism of others had more to do with Ramsey's cerebral approach to football than any serious attempt to pass the buck.

It may be harsh to criticise Rowe, when nobody but Bill Nicholson can eclipse his achievements at White Hart Lane, but with hindsight it can be seen that the fading of Rowe's team had an air of inevitability about it. This must be put into perspective, though. It is the hardest task of any manager to break up a winning eleven and start to replace them, and only the very greatest managers, such as Matt Busby, Bill Shankly, Alex Ferguson and Arsene Wenger, are able to remould successful sides into equally great, yet completely different outfits.

That FA Cup heartbreak seemed to start a downturn for Tottenham, and in the following three seasons they flirted with relegation. As if further evidence was needed of their decline, it was provided in another FA Cup shocker, this time against Third Division (North) York in the fifth round in February 1955. Despite falling behind early on, York fought back to win 3-1 and created the shock of the season. It was described in the press as a 'giantkilling' and it effectively killed the Tottenham career of manager Arthur Rowe, who was taken ill soon afterwards and was unable to resume. He retired, thus allowing his sidekick Jimmy Anderson to take control, with Bill Nicholson moving into the role of coach.

It should not be suggested that Arthur Rowe's managerial career ended in failure. In December 1954 he had set in place the foundation stone on which the 'double' side was built. Rowe always knew that it was important to sprinkle his side with intelligent, free-thinking players like

Ramsey and Nicholson, and now he single-mindedly sought the right-half he needed. Aston Villa's Danny Blanchflower cost Spurs a record £30,000 for a player in that position, though in retrospect it looked a bargain. Full credit to Rowe and the Tottenham board for snatching Blanchflower from under the noses of Arsenal. Rowe knew that a manager's contribution effectively ends when the referee's whistle starts a game, and that teams need players who can read the ebb and flow of a game and adjust tactics accordingly. Players will willingly respond to someone who talks in an honest and common sense way and who is sensitive and clever enough to pander to their individual quirks. Blanchflower effectively assumed a managerial and coaching role on the pitch, but that was only half the reason for his effectiveness.

Players are unlikely to respect those who only talk a good game, which is why sports writers and supporters are never going to be invited to manage a football club. Blanchflower was able to think about and play the game to the same high standard. This ability to adapt his game to suit the conditions, then coax his fellow professionals to do the same, provided the fulcrum which eventually helped lever Spurs into a dominant position – though six years of patience was required first.

Rowe's long-term intention had been to build a new side around Blanchflower and inside-forward Tommy Harmer, who lived up to his nickname of 'Harmer the Charmer' by becoming the fans' favourite, though he was built more like a jockey than a footballer. Rowe's ill-health put paid to that plan, and now Anderson took control.

The pushers and runners had now largely departed. Peter Murphy was the first to go, sold to Birmingham City for £20,000 in January 1952. He went on to shine in probably their best ever side, but is probably more well-known as the player who collided with Manchester City goalkeeper Bert Trautmann in the 1956 FA Cup final, thereby breaking the German keeper's neck, a shocking injury that wasn't discovered until after the match. Murphy later had a spell with Rugby Town, before eventually becoming a rep for Davenport's brewery.

Next to depart was Les Medley. At the end of 1952-53 he moved back to Canada, but by 1958 was settled in Randfontein in South Africa, where he fulfilled the role of player-coach for three years.

By this time the first of the future double-winners were on board. Peter Baker was born in Hampstead in December 1931 and was playing for Enfield in the Athenian League when Spurs came a-calling in 1952. He became understudy to Alf Ramsey, making odd appearances when his mentor was injured or called up for internationals. Ramsey's departure in 1955 should have been the springboard to a regular right-back place for

Baker, but in that first season he was often third choice for the No 2 shirt. It took time before he overcame his nerves to turn in a succession of consistent performances. This was especially important because it was Baker who was left to man the barricades whenever Danny Blanchflower set off on his attacking sorties. Baker frequently found himself without adequate defensive cover and could easily get caught out of position if he wasn't careful. He wasn't showy and this Brylcreemed blond player is often forgotten when people reminisce about the double side, though full-backs are rarely billed as stars anyway. He was one of the few players from that side who weren't accorded national honours.

There was soon a steady stream of departures from the old championship-winning side. In May 1954 Ron Burgess returned to South Wales to become Swansea Town's player-coach, then a year later, their manager. He kept them in the Second Division, and then in 1959 took charge of Watford, lifting them out of the Fourth Division. In May 1963 it was Hendon's turn to benefit from his experience, then Bedford Town's. He later scouted for Luton, before leaving football to work as a stock controller and warehouseman.

In December 1954 Les Bennett joined West Ham as a player, but not long afterwards became manager of Romford, then Clacton. Eddie Baily joined Port Vale in January 1956, then Nottingham Forest and Leyton Orient, where he became player-coach. Bill Nicholson recalled him to the Spurs fold in October 1963 as assistant manager, a role that Baily filled with notable success for eleven years until the end of Nicholson's reign. He then scouted for West Ham. Sadly he is no longer with us.

Harry Clarke remained with Spurs as a player-coach in 1957, and then became Llanelli's player-manager in February 1959. He became the third ex-push and runner (after Bennett and Ditchburn) to take charge of Romford, but eventually became an officer in a security firm.

Colin Brittan and Len Duquemin both quit Spurs to join Bedford in November 1958. Brittan had been assigned to replace both Burgess and Nicholson in various Tottenham sides, a daunting task for anyone to fulfil. The emergence of Marchi and Blanchflower had pushed him back into the reserves by the time he left. Duquemin's influence had waned too, particularly after the signing of Bobby Smith. After Bedford, he went to Hastings, then Romford. Following his retirement from football he ran a newsagents, then a pub in Cheshunt called 'The Haunch of Venison', which had nothing to do with the Liverpool player, Barry.

The last player to leave was Ted Ditchburn, who clung onto his status as the 'number one' No 1 until John Hollowbread's flowering in 1958-59. Ted wasn't finished as a player though, because after managing Romford he was seen occasionally between the sticks for Brentwood Town in the 1965-66 season, aged 44. He ran a sports shop in Romford that still bears his name today, though he no longer runs it.

Before Rowe's reign came to an end, three more double-winning stars joined the ranks. In addition to the irrepressible Blanchflower, also making their debuts during 1954-55 were Ron Henry and Terry Dyson.

Henry was born in Shoreditch in August 1934 and was an outside-left when Tottenham signed him after he completed his National Service. It took a while for his natural position to become apparent (he was tried at centre-half and left-half) and only made sporadic appearances in his first five seasons because Mel Hopkins dominated his favoured position, left-back. When Hopkins succumbed to long-term injury in 1959 (he broke his nose in an international), Henry took his chance and cemented himself in the side with a series of swashbuckling displays that showed his full range of tackling, positioning, and passing. When Hopkins regained fitness it was his turn to be frozen out of the picture. Whereas his right-sided partner, Baker, looked more urbane, Henry cut a more menacing figure on the pitch with a swarthier appearance.

Terry Dyson's appearance was anything but menacing, because he was only 5ft 3in tall. His dad was a professional jockey, but young Terry (born in Malton, Yorkshire in November 1934) decided to concentrate on his football with non-league Scarborough. He joined Tottenham in 1954, but never established himself prior to the double season because Terry Medwin and Cliff Jones held sway. If we can adopt horse racing analogies, then Dyson was a lively colt, galloping all over the field and endearing himself to the crowd for his workrate, even if his managers would sometimes tear their hair out at his frequent displays of over-confidence. Never shy to come forward, he possessed a wicked shot and was the joker in the pack as far as harassed opposition defenders were concerned.

Arthur Rowe's contract only expired in 1956, so presumably he could have returned to the manager's chair if his health has recovered sufficiently. It didn't, at first, so Rowe stood down, but he recovered enough in mind and body to become West Brom's coach in July 1957. In October 1958 he began a long association with Crystal Palace by becoming assistant manager to George Smith. Then, in April 1960, he replaced him as manager. Rowe showed he had lost none of his old abilities by leading Palace to promotion from the Fourth Division, rather appropriately during the 1960-61 season. But history repeated itself when a run of poor form led to his resignation through ill-health in November 1962.

Rowe recovered, and four months later became general manager of Palace. He even had one final fling as caretaker manager between January and April 1966. He returned to assistant manager duties until May 1971 and at one point was also director of the club. In November 1969 Palace awarded him a testimonial to celebrate his 40 years in football. Fittingly, Sir Alf Ramsey was guest of honour.

Between May and December 1971 Rowe was secretary of the short-lived 'Football Hall of Fame', then wound down his career by becoming a footballing consultant with Orient and Millwall. He retired to his home at Norbury and passed away on 8th November 1993.

Jimmy Anderson's reign as Tottenham boss (1955-58) is diminished because he was sandwiched between the two giant figures of Rowe and Nicholson. This is unfair, because he transformed a side haunted by fears of relegation into one which finished second in 1956-57 and third the following season – though it must be admitted that they finished well short of the respective champions, Manchester United, and Wolves. The Red Devils finished eight points clear of Spurs and it is probable that – were it not for the tragic events at Munich, which cost the lives of so many of that young team – United might have become the first team to win the double in the twentieth century, and the first team to win a European competition, thus eclipsing the achievements of Nicholson's side. We shall never know..

Anderson gradually shored up the Tottenham team, and in his first season introduced a couple of giants (both metaphorically and literally) into the Lilywhite set-up. Maurice Norman was born in May 1934 and was raised on the family farm at Bracon Ash, near Norwich. He spent a couple of seasons with Norwich City before joining Spurs in a player-exchange deal with Johnny Gavin, with £18,000 used as an extra sweetener for the Canaries. Somewhat surprisingly, his huge presence (at 6ft 1in he fulfils the stereotyped image of a Norfolk farmer) wasn't immediately linked with central defence. Instead he was tried out in both full-back positions, before slotting into his more natural berth as centre-half. He was powerful in the air, of course, but was intimidating to attackers on the ground, even though he was not a tackler in the Dave Mackay mould. Norman was perhaps closer to Bobby Moore in style, and fittingly it was Maurice who held the England defence together 23 times between 1962 and 1964 before Moore took over with such devastating effect.

The other big man was Bobby Smith. If it was fitting that Norman was a farmer's son, it was equally apt that Smith was sired by a Yorkshire miner. He was born in Lingdale, on the edge of the North Yorkshire Moors, in February 1933. Unconventionally, Smith's League career began with Chelsea in 1950-51 and he helped them to their only League title in 1955, though he was in the shadows of the more potent Roy Bentley at that time. Eyebrows were raised when Anderson paid Chelsea £18,000 for him in December 1955 and for the first couple of seasons Smith bagged a goal every other game, useful but unremarkable. He then found the magic touch, helped by the better quality of players providing the service, and in 1957-58 he banged 36 goals from just 38 matches. He almost equalled that the next season, and eventually overtook George Hunt's pre-War record of 124 League goals, though Jimmy Greaves in turn soon eclipsed him. Smith is fondly remembered as a good old-fashioned centre-forward, a real target man, but that image plays down the not-inconsiderable skill that was a prerequisite for any Nicholson player. Smith had a superb first touch and could juggle the ball better than many other similarly built forwards who could be downright clumsy.

The figure of £18,000 keeps reappearing as the standard transfer fee for Spurs players in the mid-1950s, and that is also how much Tottenham paid Swansea Town at the end of the 1955-56 season for Terry Medwin. He was a Swansea boy (born in September 1932) and had spent five seasons with the Welsh club, accumulating 59 League goals from his 159 games and winning three Welsh caps. His goals tally was all the more impressive because he was usually to be found patrolling the right wing, only occasionally being deployed as a forward. He was fast and skilful and grabbed many goals because he did not care which foot struck the ball: he was equally lethal with left or right. His elegant fair-haired figure was a familiar sight at the Lane in the late 1950s, though competition for his place became red-hot during the trophy-laden years.

1956-57 was a turning point for Spurs as they shook off the relegation worries of the previous three seasons and finished second, with an almost identical goals 'for and against' set of figures as the champions, Manchester United, despite being eight points adrift of the Busby Babes. Inside-forwards Tommy Harmer and Johnny Brooks were at their peak, and other players whose abilities didn't last into the 1960s were also shining. Men like left-winger George Robb and the mercurial goal-getter Alfie Stokes have been almost forgotten outside of London N17, but remain critical links in the build-up to the success of the later side.

The 1957-58 season was also gratifyingly successful, with Anderson steering his team to third place. Wolverhampton claimed the title from Busby's Munich-ravaged side, but Wolves' style owed nothing to that which the Red Devils had aspired to, or Tottenham's own title side. Instead, Stan Cullis's Wolves harked back to an earlier, darker age of long balls and incessant ball-chasing.

In the latter part of that season Anderson added another gem to Tottenham's impressive cluster of diamonds. Cliff Jones was another

Swansea boy (born February 1935) and had attained legendary status in Wales by winning his first cap at the age of eighteen in 1954. By the time Spurs splashed out £35,000 for him (a record at the time for a winger), he had already played eleven times for his country and he was still only just turning 23. Jones's footballing education was aided by having a father (Ivor) and an uncle (Bryn) who also attained international status.

Cliff Jones was an astonishing player. Able to play on either wing, he demolished defences as effectively as the big bad wolf did with paper houses. He was scintillatingly fast, amazingly skilful, and the best header of a ball that Bobby Moore was ever to come across, but he was only 5ft 7in tall. As if this wasn't enough, he was blessed with a win-at-all-costs attitude that drove him and his team-mates relentlessly in search of victory. His bravery was never, ever questioned.

Jones broke his leg pre-season, which helps to explain why Tottenham got off to a shocking start in 1958-59. It was also the last season that featured Ditchburn in goal, also because of injury. It was now apparent that a burned-out Anderson had taken Spurs as far as he could, which was a considerable distance. Anderson was the kind of manager who was more at home in the office, delegating coaching into the more-than-capable hands of Bill Nicholson, who had honed his charges into a fitter, more skilful, more tactically aware group of players. Such vision soon paid dividends as Nicholson reaped the rewards of all his hard work on the training pitch and on the blackboard.

So Nicholson was the obvious choice to take over the managerial reins. He knew the club and its players inside out. He knew what it took to win a championship and he had learned many lessons from great thinkers of the game, not only here, but abroad as well. As well as his spell in Hungary, and his club career with Rowe and Ramsey, Nicholson had also helped Walter Winterbottom coach the England set-up, and he acknowledged that this largely unsung England boss was another great source of inspiration to him.

Most managers have a 'honeymoon period' but Nicholson's first game took the footballing cliché to a new level when Spurs obliterated Everton 10-4 at White Hart Lane on 11th October 1958. It couldn't last. The team went into a spin which left them just three places above the relegation zone. The problems within the club came to a head when Nicholson axed Blanchflower, dismissing him as a 'luxury in a struggling side'. Eventually it all got sorted out and Blanchflower returned, because he was an essential item that such a team could not afford to be without. There were few things to cheer that season, but Nicholson's first capture, Dave Mackay, was cause for a celebratory jiggle in the street.

Tottenham Hotspur: Champions of England

THE SPURS OF 1950

PORTRAITS, ACTION PICTURES AND BIOGRAPHIES OF THE PLAYERS AND OFFICIALS

PRICE 1/6

This yearly publication was about to become something to treasure for posterity

ARSENAL FOOTBALL CLUB, Ltd.   85
This portion to be retained.

ARSENAL STADIUM,
HIGHBURY, N.5.

Football League, Div. I.
ARSENAL v. TOTTENHAM H.
SATURDAY, 26th, AUGUST, 1950
Kick off 3.15 p.m.

WEST STAND
HIGHBURY HILL.
(*See Map on back*)

RESERVED SEAT
10/6
(including Tax)

Block **X**
Row **N**
SEAT 124

A late penalty at Highbury earned Arsenal a 2-2 draw in this match with Tottenham

66   TOTTENHAM HOTSPUR: CHAMPIONS OF ENGLAND

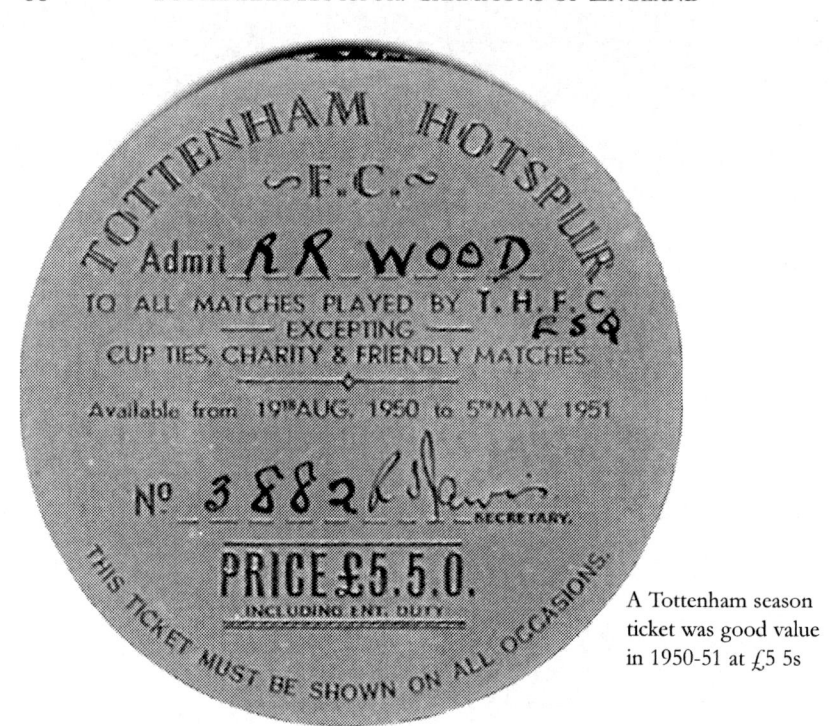

A Tottenham season ticket was good value in 1950-51 at £5 5s

This is the other side of the plastic disc given to all season ticket holders

Arthur Rowe dreams of the League and FA Cup 'double' before this Boxing Day 1950 game against Derby County. Tottenham would have to wait another ten years for the double

From left: Les Bennett, Ron Burgess, Harry Clarke and Ted Ditchburn

This thrilling and controversial 3-2 win for Tottenham against Aston Villa
would have been worth paying 10 shillings (50p) to see

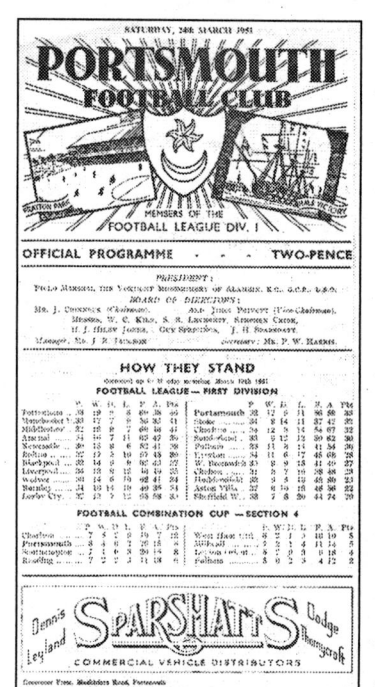

The Portsmouth programme of March 1951
shows how they surrendered their League title

Tottenham's match programme v Sheffield Wednesday in April 1951.
This was the match that clinched Spurs' first League Championship

70 TOTTENHAM HOTSPUR: CHAMPIONS OF ENGLAND

Above: The menu for Tottenham's celebration banquet in June 1951

Arthur Rowe and Ron Burgess congratulate each other before the visit of FC Austria in May 1951

Spurs' first Championship side, 1950-51. Future manager Bill Nicholson is bottom left

This image details how Les Bennett scored against Bolton (September 1951)

Sonny Walters (furthest from the camera) celebrates his goal v Wolves (November 1951). The beaten goalkeeper is Bert Williams

Wolves' Bert Williams saves from Bennett. Walters is in the centre (November 1951)

Ted Ditchburn saves from Newcastle's George Robledo.
Alf Ramsey is Spurs' No 2 and Ralph Wetton is No 4 (December 1951)

Newcastle go close. Ditchburn is the goalie and Clarke the defender (December 1951)

Les Medley jumps for the ball ahead of Newcastle's Bobby Cowell (December 1951)

Ted Ditchburn tips over v Derby. Alf Ramsey guards a post. Charlie Withers is No 3.
(March 1952)

Bennett heads goal number 3 v Derby. County's goalkeeper is Ray Middleton
(March 1952)

Tottenham Hotspur: Champions of England

A near miss for Eddie Baily. West Brom's goalkeeper is Norman Heath (August 1952)

Les Duquemin challenges against West Brom.
Goalkeeper Norman Heath prepares to intercept (August 1952)

76 TOTTENHAM HOTSPUR: CHAMPIONS OF ENGLAND

Les Duquemin tussles with Manchester United's Bill Foulkes (September 1953)

Manchester United's Jack Rowley holds off Alf Ramsey (September 1953)

Tottenham Hotspur: Champions of England

Spurs' goalkeeper Ron Reynolds saves from Sunderland's Ted Purdon, watched by Alf Ramsey (March 1954)

Eddie Baily v Sheffield United (probably April 1954)

Sonny Walters gets in a shot ahead of Wolves' Bill Shorthouse (August 1954)

Sonny Walters is tackled by Chelsea's Stan Willemse (October 1955)

TOTTENHAM HOTSPUR: CHAMPIONS OF ENGLAND 79

A young Bobby Smith lets fly against Sheffield United (April 1956)

Ted Ditchburn saves from Newcastle's Vic Keeble (November 1956)

Ditchburn and Baker clear a Sunderland attack (February 1957)

TOTTENHAM HOTSPUR Football Club

FIXTURES

SEASON 1960-61

A publication to whet the appetite of any Tottenham fan, ahead of the double-winning season

Tottenham Hotspur: Champions of England 81

Terry Dyson heads Spurs' second goal past Arsenal goalkeeper Jack Kelsey. The Gunners' No 5, John Sneddon, is motionless (September 1960)

Bobby Smith challenges Burnley goalkeeper Adam Blacklaw

TOTTENHAM HOTSPUR
Football and Athletic Company Limited

TOTTENHAM HOTSPUR
v.
MOSCOW DYNAMOS

at White Hart Lane

on MONDAY, NOVEMBER 14th, 1960

Kick-off 7.30 p.m. (floodlit)

ADMISSION PRICES
Ground 3/- (Schoolboys 1/-); Enclosure 1/6 extra; Numbered and Reserved Seats 10/- and 8/-.

TICKET RESERVATIONS
Bookings in respect of numbered and reserved seats will be accepted by POST ONLY as from MONDAY, OCTOBER 17TH, 1960. Applications cannot be accepted before this date. Block or Party bookings will be accepted as far as is practicable.

When making application the appropriate remittance must be included. Also the inclusion of a stamped and addressed envelope is of the utmost assistance to us.

SEASON TICKET HOLDERS
Season Ticket Holders will be afforded the option of purchasing their usual seat(s) BEFORE NOVEMBER 7TH and again we would ask for postal applications only commencing October 17th.
Prices of seats are as under:

OLD (WEST) STAND:	Blocks "H", "J", "K" and "L"	10/- each
	Blocks "G" and "M"	8/- each
NEW (EAST) STAND:	Blocks "C", "D", "E", "F" and "G"	10/- each
	Blocks "A", "B", "H" and "J"	8/- each

IT IS POINTED OUT THAT THIS IS NOT AN "ALL-TICKET" MATCH AND THAT GROUND ADMISSION WILL BE BY PAYMENT THROUGH THE TURNSTILES

SPECIAL NOTICE
Experience has shown that for evening matches at White Hart Lane the traffic congestion on the routes leading to Tottenham is quite considerable. Therefore we would urge all patrons to allow themselves plenty of time in order to reach the Ground at least 15 minutes before the kick-off.

This friendly confused everyone when Tottenham's opponents turned out not to be Moscow Dynamo after all, but Dynamo Tbilisi

TOTTENHAM HOTSPUR: CHAMPIONS OF ENGLAND

Bobby Smith and Danny Blanchflower exchange a joke

Charlton's Stuart Leary scores against Tottenham in the FA Cup (January 1961)

Inside-forward Les Allen was an ever-present during Spurs' 1960-61 double-winning season

Danny Blanchflower shows the new player guide to Bill Brown

TOTTENHAM HOTSPUR: CHAMPIONS OF ENGLAND

No. 526
TOTTENHAM HOTSPUR
Football & Athletic Company Ltd.
Block C   EAST STAND

TOTTENHAM HOTSPUR
v
LEICESTER CITY

On SATURDAY, FEB. 4th, 1961
Kick-off 3.00 p.m.

Row R   97
Seat No.
PRICE 8/-

The Tottenham Hotspur Company do not Guarantee that the proposed match will be played.
R. S. JARVIS
Secretary

Ticket Holders are requested to be in their seats 15 minutes at least before the Kick-off.

EAST STAND—Entrance PAXTON ROAD

Printed by Thomas Knight & Co. Ltd., The Clock House Press, Hoddesdon, Herts.

Spurs' first home defeat of the 'double' season came in this game

Spurs have just won the 1960-61 League Championship.
No wonder Danny Blanchflower is laughing in the middle of the front row

MONDAY, APRIL 17th, 1961
COPYRIGHT

VOL. LIII. NO. 47
ALL RIGHTS RESERVED

Secretary:
R. S. JARVIS

Manager:
W. E. NICHOLSON

Medical Officer:
Dr. A. E. TUGHAN

Chairman:
FRED. J. BEARMAN

Vice-Chairman:
FREDK. WALE

Directors:
F. JOHN BEARMAN, D. H. DEACOCK
S. A. WALE

TOTTENHAM HOTSPUR
FOOTBALL AND ATHLETIC COMPANY LIMITED

Official Programme
AND RECORD OF THE CLUB

VISIT OF SHEFFIELD WEDNESDAY

This evening we give a hearty welcome to Sheffield Wednesday in what is a vital fixture to both clubs in the League campaign now reaching its climax. It will be recalled that the Wednesday were the first team to defeat us this season when they won by 2 goals to 1 at Hillsborough on November 12th, and they have been in close attendance on us in the League table throughout the season, with the gap fluctuating at times with the fortunes of the clubs.

A feature of Sheffield Wednesday's performances this season has been the strength of their defence; they have conceded only 39 goals in 38 League games, a record which speaks for itself, and which represents the smallest debit total in the League. Only four times have they had more than two goals scored against them, and they won two of those matches by defeating Blackburn Rovers 5—4 at Hillsborough and Burnley 4—3 at Turf Moor.

Wednesday's away record also stamps them as a side to be accorded great respect. They have lost only three times on opponents' grounds, winning seven and drawing eight of their other 15 engagements. Their defeats were at Leicester (1—2), Wolverhampton (1—4), and Everton (2—4), with drawn games at Birmingham, West Ham, Manchester City, Blackburn and Arsenal (all 1—1). In addition to their victory at Burnley already mentioned, they have won at Cardiff, Blackpool, Bolton and Newcastle (all 1—0), Nottingham Forest (2—1) and Fulham (6—1).

The defeat at Everton on December 3rd was actually their last in a League match; since then they have gone through 19 First Division fixtures without a reverse. Their performance in doing so is all the more meritorious when it is recalled that they were involved in a coach crash on Boxing Day on their way home from Arsenal to Sheffield. Several of their players, including Peter Swan and Bobby Craig, were injured and a young reserve forward, Douglas McMillan, had to have a leg amputated. Swan received a shoulder injury which kept him out of the game for the next nine League and Cup games.

There are two ever-presents in the Hillsborough side's defence in right-back Peter Johnson and left-half Tony Kay, while right-half Tommy McAnearney has missed only two games and left-back Don Megson four, all through injury. Swan has been absent from six League matches, and goalkeeper Ron Springett—like Swan a member of the England International side—has missed four First Division games. In the attack, skipper Alan Finney has a full attendance record; he has played on both flanks of the attack, his last eight appearances having been at outside-right. At centre-forward, Keith Ellis has been the most regular choice. Three members of the attack have reached double figures as marksmen, with inside-left John Fantham leading the way with 19 League goals. Ellis has scored 14 times and Craig 12. Finney has five goals to his name, and Derek Wilkinson, who has played at outside-left in the last seven matches, after a spell on the other wing, has scored twice.

The Wednesday's last League defeat, on December 3rd, was their third reverse in consecutive games; on

---

In the Interests of Ground Conditions, Players on either side will not sign Autographs on the Field

PRICE TWOPENCE

Printed by Thomas Knight & Co. Ltd.,
The Clock House Press, Hoddesdon, Herts

The match programme for the League Championship decider of 1961.
But according to the warning on the bottom of this page, you were not
allowed to take it onto the pitch after the match to get it autographed

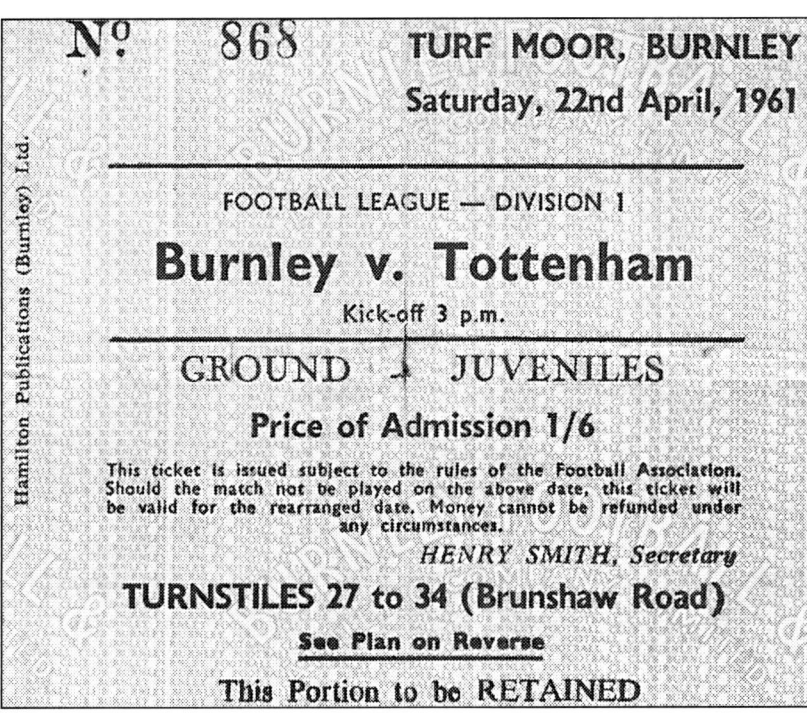

Nº 868 — TURF MOOR, BURNLEY
Saturday, 22nd April, 1961

FOOTBALL LEAGUE — DIVISION 1

Burnley v. Tottenham

Kick-off 3 p.m.

GROUND — JUVENILES

Price of Admission 1/6

This ticket is issued subject to the rules of the Football Association. Should the match not be played on the above date, this ticket will be valid for the rearranged date. Money cannot be refunded under any circumstances.

HENRY SMITH, *Secretary*

TURNSTILES 27 to 34 (Brunshaw Road)

See Plan on Reverse

This Portion to be RETAINED

Hamilton Publications (Burnley) Ltd.

Tottenham were already champions by the time of this match, and had two more home games to follow

A four-page card souvenir, published by the *Daily Express*

A SOUVENIR OF THE
F.A. CUP FINAL 1961
WEMBLEY STADIUM   SATURDAY MAY 6

WITH THE COMPLIMENTS OF THE
DAILY EXPRESS

Danny Blanchflower shows off the FA Cup at Tottenham's Town Hall (May 1961)

Win or lose, Spurs were going to celebrate after the 1961 Cup final

Left-back Ron Henry played in every game during Spurs' 1960-61 double-winning season

Whatever the weather, iron-man Dave Mackay never shirked

Danny Blanchflower

The Spurs skipper with the FA Cup

The open-topped bus carries the Tottenham players from Edmonton to Tottenham to show off the League and Cup trophies

Bill Brown advertises string vests, which were fashionable in the 1960s

Tottenham played Feyenoord and an Amsterdam XI on this tour and won both games

The unsung heroes behind the scenes at White Hart Lane enjoy
equal billing in this club photograph

Magical winger Cliff Jones scored 15
League goals for the 1961 title-winners

Centre-half Maurice Norman missed only one game during the 1960-61 double-winning season

John White, Spurs' No 8, never missed a game during the historic double-winning season

Arsenal goalkeeper John McClelland looks to be practising yoga. Bobby Smith's smile would soon be wiped off his face, as the 'goal' was disallowed (August 1961)

A Christmas card from Tottenham Hotspur in 1961 shows off the spoils of the double

The club's directors issued a printed autograph sheet every season.
This is the one to celebrate the 'double'

THE "SPURS" GO MARCHING ON

The "Spurs" Victory Song

SOUVENIR

The cover of the 1962 FA Cup final four-page card

Below: The inside pages of the four-page card distributed at the 1962 FA Cup final, complete with the famous words

THE "SPURS" GO MARCHING ON

Words by Eric James.   Music arranged from an American Marching Song by Eric James.

We had some famous Football teams
In England thro' the years.
From North and South,
From East and West.
The Midlands had our cheers.
There is a team from London town
Their record crowns the years.
The "Spurs" go marching on
Glory, Glory, Halleluyah.
The "Spurs" go marching on.

Their fame will live forever,
And their name will never die.
The team, Brown, Baker, Henry,
Blanchflower, Norman and Mackay.
Jones, White, Smith, Allen, Dyson.
Raise your voices to the sky.
The "Spurs" go marching on.
Glory, Glory, Halleluyah.
The "Spurs" go marching on.

Nineteen-o-one they won the cup
And again in twenty one.
In fifty and in fifty one
League Championships they won
And then they won the "Double"
League, and cup in sixty one.
The "Spurs" go marching on.
Glory, Glory, Haleluyah.
The "Spurs" go marching on.

The Spurs who have made History
Arthur Grimsdell you all know
Ron Burgess and that architect
of football Arthur Rowe.
Danny Blanchflower and Bill Nicholson
Who made the Cockerell Crow.
The "Spurs" go marching on.
Glory, Glory, Halleluyah.
The "Spurs" go marching on.

The Ten-Year Itch (1951-60)

Mackay had been with Heart of Midlothian in his native Edinburgh for five years, during which time they had claimed all three of Scotland's domestic honours (League, League Cup and Scottish Cup). His country had also called on his services four times. Nicholson paid £32,000 for him in March 1959, which many regarded as a gamble at the time, but the left-half repaid that back many times over. In fact, Tottenham nearly did not get his services at all, because Nicholson's first choice was Swansea's Mel Charles, who opted to join Arsenal instead. It's not denigrating the fine Charles in the slightest to declare that this was a critical piece of good fortune for Spurs.

A manager can buy eleven great players, but there is no guarantee that they will blend as a single unit. Mackay slotted into the team like a dream, because he formed a natural relationship with Blanchflower. It is often stated that Mackay was the heart of midfield, whilst Blanchflower was the brains, but that doesn't do justice to either player. Mackay, like his colleague, had a tremendous will to win that drove him on when others were starting to flag, but his game wasn't all about power and energy – he was without doubt the most skilful ball-player in the team, able to perform tricks with the ball that left his fellow professionals gaping, such as repeatedly volleying against a wall from twelve yards, without allowing the ball to hit the ground, and doing it up to 36 times. Tottenham fans used to focus on him as the teams ran out onto the pitch, because he would always do something outrageous, that he knew the opposition players were incapable of, like hitting the ball high into the air and nonchalantly trapping it with his instep. Mackay knew that football was as much a mind game as a physical one.

Certainly Mackay was well-equipped physically. Try to imagine him, and it's easy to remember him as a six-footer, but in reality he was only 5ft 8in. With a barrel chest sticking out, he could frighten anybody simply with his passion. Remember the famous photograph of a simpering Billy Bremner being grabbed by his shirt by a furious Mackay?

The 1959-60 League Championship race was one of the most remarkable in history. Wolves galloped away and looked to have it all wrapped up going into the final furlong. As Wolves had won the title the two previous seasons and had also reached the 1960 Cup final against a mediocre Blackburn side, they seemed destined to become the first team of the century to achieve the League and Cup double. They did indeed win the FA Cup, but their championship dreams lay in tatters when Tottenham beat them 3-1 at Molineux in their penultimate League game. This should have put the title in Tottenham's hands, except that they had unaccountably lost their last two home games, enabling Burnley to come from nowhere to poke their noses in front. It was heartbreaking for Spurs at the time, but with hindsight it drove them on to make history the following season. How sweet that it was Tottenham who should thwart an Old Gold double and therefore not allow next season's exploits to be diminished in any way.

The last three cogs in the Nicholson gearbox were put in place in that season. With Ditchburn gone, John Hollowbread had taken over the green jersey, only to be left shell-shocked when Bill Brown was signed from Dundee for £16,500 in the summer of 1959. At nearly 28 years old, in those days that was regarded as an advanced age for a goalkeeper, but Brown possessed all the attributes needed, except an ability to pluck out crosses, which did not really matter as Maurice Norman was expert in heading them away. Also, Brown was quieter than most goalkeepers, preferring not to bellow instructions at his defenders, instead relying on gentle persuasion. He was tall, and very slim, which enabled him to contort his body into some remarkable positions when making saves. This slenderness may have been due to his chain smoking, which nullified the effects of an equally remarkable liking for food. Brown also had an aversion to throwing the ball out, preferring to kick it accurately to a colleague instead.

Another Nicholson signing that initially baffled supporters was yet another Scot. John White was born in Musselburgh in April 1937 and played for Alloa Athletic and Falkirk. A hefty £20,000 was given to the Bairns' chairman in exchange for 22-year-old White in October 1959, an amazing sum for a Scottish Second Division player. Michael Basser, a Spurs fan, well remembers the reaction when the new signing ran out on the pitch for the first time. 'He seemed about five feet four inches tall, seven stone, and looked more like a mascot than a player. I wondered what on earth Nicholson had done by signing such a player. After ten minutes I found out why.'

Rangers, Charlton and Middlesbrough had been deterred by White's willowy physique, but Nicholson wasn't, discovering that White was an accomplished cross-country runner, and therefore had the stamina required for a 90-minute workout on the pitch. His long-distance running ability gave him a silky-smooth gait that made it seem as though he was materialising from nowhere. This uncanny ability to steal into dangerous positions earned him the tag of 'The Ghost of White Hart Lane', as White hared around the right-hand side of the pitch. He was a workaholic and it was said that the ball would have to beg before he would release it, and then inevitably it would be floated over towards a hungry forward. As games neared their conclusion and 21 pairs of legs started to tire, it was then that White would come into his own as his extra energy made itself known.

The final part of Nicholson's plan appeared in December 1959, when he swapped Johnny Brooks for Les Allen, in a deal with Chelsea. Allen had fallen out of favour at Stamford Bridge, but the Tottenham boss was confident he could bring the best out of the Dagenham-born 22-year-old forward. Allen got off to a great start by bagging five goals in the 13-2 thrashing of Crewe in an FA Cup replay, but lost form towards the end of the season. More than most, he was prone to losing confidence easily, allowing plenty of one-on-one chances to go begging. When he was on form he was unstoppable, tirelessly teeing up Bobby Smith if he couldn't score himself.

Tommy Harmer was winding down his Tottenham career, effectively usurped by White, and the only other player so far unmentioned. Tony Marchi had been despatched to Lanerossi in Italy in 1957, only to return to Tottenham in August 1959 for a £20,000 fee from Juventus (he played for Torino in between). Marchi's sheer versatility counted against him, though, and he failed to make any one position his own, slotting in whenever injury ruled out a regular. If substitutes had been allowed then he might have been a perpetual No 12.

Chapter 6

~ THE PERFECT START ~

(August-November 1960)

In the summer of 1960 the Spurs players underwent a tough pre-season workout with particular attention paid to what roles individual players were expected to fulfil. By now, Bill Nicholson was sure in his own mind exactly how he wanted his men to go about their business. Given that most of the team were already fulfilling that brief, it was more a question of fine-tuning the system rather than unloading a new set of tactics. To emphasise this, much time was spent working on set-pieces, such as free-kicks and corners, and this undoubtedly paid dividends once the season was under way.

The season kicked off with the traditional practice curtain-raiser between the Whites (first team) and the Blues (reserves). Just 11,677 turned up for the spectacle, approximately 5,000 down on the previous season, a drop which was blamed on there being no new players to inspect. The lack of fresh blood made it easier for Nicholson to select his first-choice eleven, his problem being how to juggle the positions of those eleven players. Dave Mackay moved back into a more defensive left-half role, whilst Les Allen had a chance to stake his claim for a regular place once again, following a disappointing loss of form towards the end of the previous campaign.

If the manager and supporters were unsurprised by the way the first team strolled into a 4-1 lead, they must have been delighted at the ability of the reserves, who stormed back to level with three goals in the final twenty minutes. Players of the calibre of Tommy Harmer (inside-right), Mel Hopkins (right-back) and John Hollowbread (goalkeeper) had featured in the first team for years, but were now in the reserves. It was gratifying to see the way new boys like sixteen-year-old Frank Saul and right-winger Barry Aitchison blended in with them. On this performance, Spurs had every position covered by a capable understudy. Some First Division managers might have swapped their first teams for Spurs' second. This game firmly locked a simple fact into every first-teamer's mind. If they didn't perform, someone was straining to replace them.

It had been hoped that Tottenham could play five-times European Cup-winners Real Madrid at the start of the season, but the Spanish club

The Perfect Start *(August-November 1960)*

faced too many commitments. The two clubs had met in a friendly back in September 1925, with Spurs winning 4-0, but no room could now be found on either club's crowded schedules, which was a pity.

Everton provided the opening-day opponents on 20th August 1960, and provided an interesting test at White Hart Lane. The Toffeemen had featured in the bottom half of the table for the last five seasons, and were still mindful of the 4-10 drubbing Spurs had dished out in October 1958, but now they had bought themselves a decent side, using the money of Pools magnate John Moores. His inexhaustible funds appeared to have been spent wisely by manager Johnny Carey, because their defence held firm against the concerted and imaginative attacks of the home team. With Tottenham's defence also looking impregnable, for 86 minutes it looked like a goalless draw was going to be marked on everyone's Pools coupon that Saturday. Les Allen recalls it as being the only game of the season where the White Hart Lane crowd were obviously frustrated and let their feelings be known to the players. Then came the breakthrough. Bobby Smith spotted a gap in the blue wall and sprinted through it, only to be clattered down inside the penalty area. Referee Crawford was astute enough to allow the advantage, because the ball fell to Les Allen who toe-poked it home. With the tension lifted, Spurs were able to add a second goal, when John White sent over a cross that was spectacularly converted by the horizontally diving Smith. That 2-0 win sent Tottenham to the top of the table, and though it is largely an academic exercise to construct it after only one game, it did give Spurs the satisfaction of leading the way from the word go, though everyone was aware that they hadn't played well enough that day to satisfy the manager.

The season commenced on a Bank Holiday, so on the Monday Spurs travelled north to Blackpool, giving some fans the excuse for a short seaside break before watching the football. No doubt many of the crowd of 27,656 were curious holidaymakers, and they were rewarded with a game that rivalled any attractions that the Golden Mile could provide. This time Spurs made hay early on, and John White was again the provider with another killer cross that was firmly dispatched. The only surprise was the identity of the goalscorer – ex-jockey Terry Dyson launched himself vertically over Blackpool's much taller defenders. The home side should have equalised, but Kaye sent his penalty kick wide after Peter Baker had clumsily chopped down Ray Charnley. That miss was to prove costly as Tottenham clicked into another gear in the second half. Terry Medwin, who had taken the place of an injured Cliff Jones, drove home their crucial second goal, and then Baker made up for his penalty blunder by teeing up Dyson for the third. Blackpool did pull one back, but it was in vain. Given that many teams were not playing that day, Spurs now strode two points clear of the pack.

One of those teams also registering an opening-day success was Blackburn Rovers. They had whacked Manchester United 3-1 at Old Trafford, so were a serious proposition, at least until they took to the field at Ewood Park. A sharp shower wetted the pitch, but it was Spurs who whetted the appetite as they killed the game in a mere seventeen minutes. Long-standing Spurs fans were instantly transported back ten years as the modern side proved they could 'push and run' as well as the old-timers had. Quick, slick interchanges bypassed the mentally and physically pedestrian Rovers' players. Bobby Smith capitalised by stroking home the opening goal, then executed a textbook header from Mackay's free-kick. The third goal swiftly followed. Blanchflower to Dyson, Dyson to Allen, Allen to goal. It was a magnificent display, made even more memorable by the fact that the defence held firm as Blackburn desperately tried to rescue themselves from the wreckage that had been wrought upon them. Norman orchestrated the back line, whilst Brown resembled a violin bow as he flung himself this way and that across the goalmouth. With any chance of a comeback scotched, Spurs were able to add a fourth when Allen returned an earlier favour by teeing up Dyson with the easiest of goals. Blackburn did manage to score in the closing seconds but that did little to ease their pain.

Blackpool's manager Ronnie Suart must have muttered dark threats against the fixture compilers, who had decreed that his side had to play rampant Tottenham twice in the first four games. His fears would hardly have been assuaged when he learnt that Bobby Smith was seeking one goal to carry him above the record 138 League and Cup goals set by Tottenham stalwart George Hunt in the 1930s. Smith took just four minutes to eclipse that record with a smart header, but then Blackpool decided to make a game of it. They gained a merited equaliser ten minutes before the break, before testing a resolute Spurs defence with yet more attacks. The home defence breathed a sigh of relief, along with the majority of the 45,000 White Hart Lane crowd, when Messrs Dyson and Medwin laid on efforts for Smith that the front man greedily gobbled up to earn himself a hat-trick. Curiously, the Barcelona team popped into White Hart Lane, but being as they arrived late and left early, they never got to see any Tottenham goals. No matter, that fourth straight win kept Spurs a point clear of Sheffield Wednesday and Wolves, who had each drawn a game along the way.

The next item on the agenda was a 3rd September meeting with Manchester United that succeeded in putting an extra 10,000 on the gate,

The Perfect Start *(August-November 1960)*

bringing it up to 55,445. Matt Busby had rebuilt his Red Devils after the horror of Munich, but his team still needed strengthening in order to reach its potential, particularly the defence, whose weaknesses had largely wiped out the advantages gained by their fearful attack. This failing had carried on in the opening games of this season, with the added disadvantage of a stuttering attack to go with it. The only time the forward line had gelled properly, against neighbours Manchester City, the game had been abandoned due to a waterlogged pitch.

Spurs had already proved themselves capable of breaking open tight defences, as a master safecracker might unpick a seemingly impregnable lock. When given the chance to work their magic against a porous defence, they set about their task with glee. Maurice Setters demonstrated United's frailties after seven minutes when he attempted a square ball across his defence to nobody in particular. John White pounced and Smith raced in for the kill. Les Allen made it 2-0 after twenty minutes by single-handedly dodging all attempts to stop him. Manchester United still had a team of great individuals, even if they weren't meshing together, and their most dangerous player, Dennis Viollet, pulled a goal back before half-time. Spurs raised their game yet higher in the second half and turned it into a rout by adding further goals from Allen and Smith. That 4-1 whipping left poor United just three places off the bottom of the table.

Cliff Jones was still absent from the team due to a badly bruised ankle sustained on the opening day. Now Bobby Smith joined him in the treatment room. Frank Saul, just seventeen, who had only turned professional the month before, took Smith's place in attack. It was certainly a gamble by Nicholson, but it underlined a potential weakness in the Spurs set-up. Smith was about the only player without an obvious replacement, should he get injured or lose form, and he had gone off the boil at the end of the previous season. Eddie Clayton was usually brought in during times of need, but Saul won Nicholson's heart following some good performances in the reserves. Young Saul made his debut at Burnden Park in a rare Wednesday evening fixture, but when Bolton took a shock third-minute lead through a deflected shot, the gamble looked to have failed. Surely Spurs needed proven ability and a wise head to inspire the fight back. For an hour that was the case, even though Saul did hit a post with one effort, but the game turned Tottenham's way when Bolton's left-back was crocked. The visitors had found it hard going against eleven men, but against a team effectively reduced to ten in the last half-hour, they were able to make the man advantage count, which is usually far from a formality. Tottenham's smart passing, which utilised the full extent of the pitch, was the key to it all. Poor Bolton found it impossible to keep tabs on all the players surging forward and they lost their lead when Allen headed in Medwin's cross. The second goal was refreshingly different. Blanchflower lobbed the Trotters' defence and White finished the job off. That made it six wins out of six and already the top three clubs had opened up a gap on the following pack.

	P	W	D	L	F	A	Pts
SPURS	6	6	0	0	18	5	12
Wolves	6	5	1	0	16	8	11
Sheffield Wed	6	4	2	0	7	2	10
Arsenal	6	3	1	2	8	5	7
Manchester C	5	2	3	0	8	5	7

On 10th September, Tottenham made the short journey from N17 to N5 in order to play their great rivals. It was in 1956-57 that both north London sides had finished in the top five together. Since then, one club tended to enjoy relative success while the other floundered in the bottom half. Apart from the aberration of 1958-59, when Spurs flirted rather too keenly with the two relegation places, it had tended to be Arsenal who were on the receiving end. Tottenham's record in derby games was less happy. Since the championship success of 1950-51, Tottenham's League record against Arsenal made grim reading:

	P	W	D	L	F	A	Pts
Tottenham	18	5	3	10	27	40	13

Clearly the hoodoo that their neighbours exerted over them had to be exorcised in order for Spurs to keep up a realistic championship bid.

Young Saul retained his place, as Smith was still out of action, but any fears that Spurs fans may have had over the inclusion of the nipper were removed when he showed his ability after a dozen minutes had ticked by on the giant Highbury clock. Neatly beating a couple of defenders, he let loose with a powerful shot that Jack Kelsey barely saw. Saul also played a key role in the second goal, which illustrated a move that had been practised in training. Mackay wound up his arms to deliver a mighty long throw to the near post, Saul back-headed it, and Dyson stole in at the far post to make it 2-0. Tottenham wasted further chances to seal the victory, but as the game progressed into the last half-hour it didn't seem to matter. Until that is, Arsenal pulled a goal back. It may have been a scrappy affair from a corner, but it lifted the red and white players and five minutes later they were level when Gerry Ward volleyed in a screamer from 25 yards. Even the stunned Spurs fans found themselves involuntarily applauding what looked like the goal of the season so far.

That equaliser set off alarm bells within the white and blue ranks and six minutes later Spurs regained their lead. Blanchflower heaved a long punt over the Arsenal defence and Allen latched onto it to score. Arsenal players and fans argued long and hard about its validity, claiming that Allen was offside, but the effort stood and it proved to be the winning goal.

That 3-2 win looked close on paper and an analysis of the match statistics seemed to confirm this. The corner-kick count was 6-5 in Arsenal's favour, whilst they also edged out Spurs on shots at goal – 19-18. This only proved that statistics can lie. In reality, most of Arsenal's efforts were from long range, and so wide that Brown was relatively untroubled. Tottenham tended to shoot from nearer in, and were more accurate, so Jack Kelsey was a busy boy. Even ardent Gunners fans were forced to admit that it had been a victory by a team over a collection of individuals. Even so, it was played in a fair spirit and at the end Dave Mackay and Tommy Docherty were able to embrace each other as fellow Scots rather than implacable enemies.

Seven straight League wins equalled a Spurs record set forty years previously – in the Second Division Championship campaign. That sequence had included two wins over the long-forgotten South Shields, and the first dropped point – in the eighth game – had come at Lincoln City. Spurs now had to overcome Bolton at home to set a new mark, and this they duly did by the scoreline of 3-1. Smith was fit once more and reclaimed his place from Saul, and celebrated his recall by cracking in a couple of goals. Also making a comeback was Cliff Jones on the right wing, though he still wasn't completely match fit. This was demonstrated when Spurs won a penalty and Blanchflower stepped up to dispatch it, after Jones had asked his captain if he could be excused the task.

Eight straight wins highlighted the fact that Nicholson had eleven players who were going to be selected week in and week out, as long as they were free of injuries. The downside was that Tottenham's reserves now regularly fielded star players without any hope of displacing their more highly-favoured colleagues. John Hollowbread, Tony Marchi, Terry Medwin, Mel Hopkins, John Hills and Tommy Harmer were once first-team regulars, but were now definitely second-best. One group of discontented players even went so far as to write to the board asking exactly where they stood. The board, unwilling to undermine Nicholson, replied that the disgruntled reserves would only make the first team if the manager decided it was appropriate. There was no question of a rotation system being employed and rumours abounded that players like Medwin and Harmer were looking for other clubs that could guarantee them first-team action. There was a suggestion of a compromise if Tottenham fielded a reserve side in the new League Cup, but Spurs had declined to enter the competition, along with many other top sides, citing it as an unwelcome distraction from the only two domestic competitions worth winning – the Football League and the FA Cup.

A trip to Leicester was the next item on the agenda for the first team (the reserves were also playing Leicester at the same time). Smith once more scored a brace of goals to take his tally to twelve in the seven games that he had played. He was now the leading striker in the division, despite some of his rivals having played an extra couple of games. This reliance on Smith hid a more worrying problem. Spurs were now so adept and comfortable in their passing game that it appeared that they were approaching matches too casually at times. They certainly spurned several opportunities to wrap up this particular game, and their 100 per cent record may well have ended prematurely had Leicester gained a second equaliser, which they so nearly did. The 2-1 win was welcome, but largely unconvincing.

A home game with Aston Villa gave Tottenham the chance to break the all-time League record of nine consecutive wins from the start of the season, set by Hull City on their way to the Third Division (North) title in 1948-49. The omens were good for Tottenham: Villa hadn't registered a League win over them since Spurs had returned to the top flight in 1950. The exciting brand of football played by the Lilywhites had now enticed the casual fans and 61,356 packed into White Hart Lane, nearly 6,000 up on the Manchester United gate, which was the previous high.

The part-time supporters picked the right game to come along. Bill Nicholson had obviously stressed the importance of turning his team's territorial advantage into goals, because they tore into a Villa side that were on paper one of the better sides in the League. John White put Spurs two goals to the good in the opening nineteen minutes, then Smith and Dyson turned the screw by making it 4-0 after only half an hour. Les Allen added a fifth in the second half, but then Villa struck twice to give the scoreline a hint of respectability. They deserved it too, because they had come close on several occasions, though goalkeeper Brown was more troubled by the uncompromising way the Villa forwards knocked him off his feet at every opportunity. Dave Mackay perhaps sensed that Spurs were lapsing into sleepwalking mode and responded by scoring his first goal of the season near the end to make it 6-2.

Wolves had briefly replaced Sheffield Wednesday as the main challengers to Tottenham's supremacy, but had subsequently won just once in five outings. Now Wolves had to face the seemingly unstoppable Spurs at Molineux. The home side hoped they could take advantage of the absence of Dave Mackay, laid low with food poisoning, but Tony Marchi was a capable replacement. Wolves had been regarded as the best side in England for three seasons, winning the Championship in 1957-58 and 1958-59 and coming extremely close to capturing the elusive double in 1959-60 before a 1-3 loss at home to Spurs allowed Burnley to pinch the League title.

For 35 minutes Wolves held the young pretenders back, but then Cliff Jones bagged his first goal of the season to once again prove that Spurs could prosper without Smith, who at that moment was writhing in agony on the halfway line, thankfully only temporarily. Now the balance of English football was tilting Tottenham's way, just as the game was. Wolves relied on an offside trap to frustrate the Tottenham forwards, but this was a feeble obstacle against a side which was master of short, sharp passing. Spurs had other ways of smashing Wolves' carefully laid plans, too, as demonstrated by Blanchflower crashing the ball into the net from 25 yards as the Wolves defence charged *en masse* towards him. There was no respite for Wolves in the second half, either, because White soon made it 3-0 and Dyson added a fourth. Gratifyingly the defence kept a clean sheet – ironically their first since the opening day of the season – though it could hardly be regarded as a weak point in the team. There just weren't any. That eleventh straight win proved that, to date, Spurs had come closer to perfection than any other English team in history. Tottenham's statistics were mightily impressive, and the First Division table was looking equally good:

	P	W	D	L	F	A	Pts
SPURS	11	11	0	0	36	11	22
Sheffield Wed	11	8	3	0	19	7	19
Everton	11	7	1	3	28	19	15
Burnley	11	7	0	4	25	15	14
Blackburn	11	6	2	3	27	20	14
Wolves	11	6	2	3	20	18	14

'I am in a very satisfactory position to address this meeting this evening.' So said the master of understatement, Bill Nicholson, at a gathering of shareholders on Monday, 3rd October. This produced a good laugh and the happy band of directors were able to pass a resolution for a celebration dinner if Spurs were to gain the League or Cup that season. They even mentioned the possibility of the double, which brought a mild admonishment from Chairman Bearman, who advised them 'not to count their chickens until they had hatched'. He also announced the financial results from the previous season, which amounted to a profit of £23,070, not a high figure considering that Spurs were the best supported team in the land. Indeed, their revenue from home and away matches was £204,710: in those days clubs split the receipts 50-50 for all games. To put it another way, Spurs needed ten fans to click through the turnstiles to earn themselves a pound in gate receipts.

Saturday 10th October was a rest day for most Spurs players, because the Football League had introduced a ruling that games could be postponed if a club had two or more players on international duty. This was somewhat fortuitous to Spurs, because they would otherwise have been denied the services of Bobby Smith and Danny Blanchflower, who lined up against one another in an England v Northern Ireland Home International Championship match. The strength of Spurs' reserves hardly made it a daunting task for Nicholson to replace these two players, but rules are rules. Anyway, it gave Smith the chance to make his England debut, and interestingly enough he got the chance to play alongside the future star who would ultimately replace him at Spurs – Chelsea's Jimmy Greaves. The pairing was a success and Smith (one goal) and Greaves (two) both scored in the 5-2 victory.

The postponed fixture was against Manchester City, and it took place two days later under the White Hart Lane floodlights. The 7.30 kick-off meant that the 59,000 supporters bound for the game had to mix it with the millions trying to get home after their day's work. The result was gridlock, with traffic stacked all the way back to Liverpool Street, nearly seven miles away. This caused problems for the Manchester City team, who had arrived at Victoria Station after spending a few days training at Eastbourne. Their coach left Victoria at 5.05pm for the ten-mile journey north. This should have taken them under an hour, but two hours later there was still no sign of them. Frantic phone calls were made to police stations *en route* to try to locate them and to belatedly organise a police escort for the remainder of the journey. Finally, at 7.20pm the coach reached White Hart Lane and the City players made a dash for the changing rooms. Incredibly, they were out on the pitch within nine minutes.

Unsurprisingly, City were slow to get going, and Tottenham swept into their usual rhythm. Allen gave Spurs the lead after 27 minutes, whilst delayed spectators were still squeezing through the turnstiles. Spurs were denied further goals by the brilliance of German veteran goalkeeper Bert

Trautmann and the premature blowing of referee Pulin's whistle for a foul on Smith, just as Allen was about to score.

Bobby Smith's knack of barging goalkeepers into the back of the net came spectacularly undone when he attempted to do it to Trautmann. The former prisoner-of-war twisted his body out of the way, leaving Smith a crumpled heap in the netting. To his credit, Smith saw the funny side and had a good laugh with Trautmann afterwards.

This time, a one-goal advantage wasn't enough. City began playing with a swagger and a confidence that matched their opponents, and equalised when Clive Colbridge smacked home Denis Law's cross. Both sides had chances to snatch a win, but it finished 1-1. So Spurs relinquished their 100 per cent record and fittingly it was City who had done the job, because it was they who had beaten Spurs at the Lane last April to end Tottenham's championship challenge.

Nicholson put the result down to the fact that his team were making diagonal passes to the wings instead of to the centre, but he was consoled by the fact that the record had gone after a great footballing display by both sides, watched by England manager Walter Winterbottom and ex-Spurs boss Arthur Rowe. Les Allen recalls that in many ways the draw was a relief, because the expectation of winning game after game was building up a mountain of pressure that was starting to take a subconscious toll on the team.

Saturday, 15th October saw over 37,000 spectators pack into the City Ground, Nottingham, to witness Spurs' clash with Forest. Tottenham were giving most clubs their highest gates when they visited, and this gate even eclipsed that at Arsenal, at home to Aston Villa. One person absent from the match was Nicholson, who took to his bed with a heavy cold. Assistant manager Harry Evans ministered to the team in his place. Spurs weren't handicapped by Nicholson's absence at all: they could probably have still romped to a 4-0 win against lowly Forest with a primary school kid in charge, because everyone instinctively knew what to do, and Blanchflower and Mackay were able to make any adaptations that were required on the field of play.

On the Wednesday, Bobby Smith travelled to Luxembourg to score a couple of goals in the 9-0 England romp, whilst the following Saturday saw another postponement for Spurs, as Hopkins and Medwin lined up for Wales against Mackay for Scotland. For right-back Mel Hopkins it was a strange occasion because he hadn't played in Tottenham's first team since shattering his nose in the previous season's Wales-Scotland encounter. Following plastic surgery to reconstruct his nose, Medwin had found it impossible to part Baker from the Spurs No 2 shirt. Now, as

Medwin trudged off the pitch following Wales' 0-3 defeat, he learned that his father Cameron had suffered a heart attack whilst watching the game. He died the following day.

Deprived of first-team action that week, Spurs hastily arranged a home friendly against an Army side for the Monday. Nicholson fielded a strong line-up, with just three inexperienced players – Dodge, Atkinson and Collins. Embarrassingly, Spurs were beaten 3-5 by the Army side that consisted of a mix of mostly young English and Scottish League players undergoing their National Service. Star performer was a giant young defender from Dundee called Ron Yeats, who impressed everyone watching. He was later to become the rock on which Bill Shankly built his fearsome Liverpool side of the mid-1960s.

Whilst the crowd of 5,947 were admiring the talents of a player who would become one of the stars of the 1960s, many more Spurs fans were raising a glass to Tommy Harmer, one of their favourite '50s heroes. He had signed professional terms for Tottenham in 1948, finally making his debut in the 1951-52 season. For five years he battled away to make the inside-right berth his own, finally achieving his objective in the resurgent side that finished as League runners-up in 1956-57. Since then, he had made 205 League appearances in the famous white and blue shirt, but had recently found it impossible to escape from the reserve team. He was regarded as a superbly talented ball-player and goal creator, one who relied on craft rather then graft. On the downside, it was felt he was too easily dispossessed by more robust opponents, and Nicholson obviously saw him as expendable. Harmer was sold to Watford for £6,000. Their manager knew all about him as it was none other than Harmer's old teammate Ronnie Burgess, who was in charge at Vicarage Road. Burgess had lifted the Hornets out of the Fourth Division the previous season, and was now trying to strengthen his side for the push towards the Second Division.

The money received from Watford was partly spent on two giant plastic sheets to protect the pitch. Nicholson had vivid memories of the unremitting rainstorms that had threatened to literally bog down the 1950-51 side's championship challenge. Now he was determined that, ten years on, his protégés were going to strut their stuff on grass, not mud. The covers did their job, because even though it was a typically wet autumn, the pitch remained firm and largely mud free, unlike Highbury, which resembled an Irish peat bog. The only problem came when trying to remove the sodden covers before a match. Both sheets had to be carefully rolled up to ensure that the water lying on top was pushed out to the edge of the pitch. The combined weight of the plastic and water ensured

The Perfect Start *(August-November 1960)*

that it was hard work for the groundstaff, and anyone foolish enough to be standing idly nearby was likely to roped in for a task that took nearly two hours to complete.

Newcastle United were the hosts for Tottenham's fourteenth match of the season, but they were hardly looking forward to it, because they had already been beaten three times on home turf this season. Nevertheless, a 51,000 crowd converged on St James' Park to witness the spectacle. For half an hour they were entertained by good, end-to-end football, but no goals were forthcoming. Then the floodgates opened and the crowd were forced to concentrate just to keep up with the score. It was the Magpies' Len White who initiated the proceedings, making a monkey out Mackay and Blanchflower as he coolly sidestepped his way round them to score. Not many players could claim to have done that in their careers. Spurs soon levelled, though. A familiar corner-kick routine saw Mackay steer Dyson's corner-kick onto the head of Norman, who nodded in.

Len White was peeved at the undoing of his fine work, and almost immediately he smashed his way through Tottenham's defence to restore the lead, which is how things stood at half-time. Soon after the restart, White's name appeared once more on the scoresheet, but this time it was John White for Tottenham. The visitors then took the lead for the first time. Cliff Jones was flagged offside as he embarked on his run to goal, and the crowd waited for the inevitable referee's whistle to disallow it. It never came.

So, 3-2 to Spurs, but Hughes levelled things with a speculative long shot that bamboozled Brown. The punch-drunk supporters were still reeling from the goal-feast, especially as there was still half an hour to play. Unsurprisingly, the breakneck pace couldn't be maintained, but still the crowd was on tenterhooks as they waited to see which way the pendulum would ultimately swing. The fact that it swung towards Spurs can be explained by the presence of goal-machine Bobby Smith. He took his tally to fifteen for the season by joyously banging in the winner.

Back at White Hart Lane, Tottenham fans were watching the reserves triumph 3-0 over Orient reserves, with Marchi, Medwin and Saul starring. Tottenham had maintained the tradition of providing a scoreboard which updated the first team's progress every fifteen minutes, and one can only imagine the oohs and aahs as the numbers were changed. Meanwhile, the third team were in action at their Cheshunt home, and they maintained their 100 per cent record in the Eastern Counties League by despatching Harwich and Parkeston 9-0.

Those Tottenham fans, by far the majority, who only attended home games had been deprived of seeing their heroes for two and a half weeks, but Wednesday, 2nd November saw Cardiff make the long trek down to London in those pre-M4 days. Tottenham were forced to make one change. Cliff Jones had been picked to represent the Football League in the 2-4 defeat against the Italian League in Milan the same night. Terry Medwin was automatically chosen to take his place.

Nicholson was certainly given material to ponder, as he witnessed his men work hard for a 3-2 victory over the struggling Welsh side. Once again Spurs were required to come from behind, and once again they were assisted by dodgy refereeing, when Cardiff's right-half Gammon appeared to handle the ball accidentally. Blanchflower's resulting penalty made it 3-1, opening up just enough of a gap to ensure Tottenham earned both points. Cardiff halved the deficit, and the 47,000 home fans were relieved to hear the final whistle.

Jones had returned from Italy with a slight knock, but Nicholson decided to play him for Saturday's home game against Fulham. It was a master move. Tottenham looked unconvincing, despite leading 1-0, when Dyson whipped in a cross that was headed in by the diving Welshman. With fifteen minutes to go, Jones supplied another diving header. Spurs had by then been pulled back to 2-1 and Jones was limping with a recurrence of his Italian injury. Tottenham were able to terrorise and torture the Cottagers in the closing minutes and racked up a 5-1 scoreline. The First Division table looked like this:

	P	W	D	L	F	A	Pts
SPURS	16	15	1	0	53	18	31
Sheffield Wed	15	10	4	1	26	11	24
Everton	16	10	3	3	38	25	23
Wolves	16	9	4	3	37	29	22

Chapter 7

~ Maintaining the Pace ~
(November 1960 – February 1961)

Already it was critical for Sheffield Wednesday to win their home game with Spurs on 12th November in order to keep their London rivals in sight. They were helped in their quest by two sets of statistics. The first was down to the Owls' defence, which had managed to restrict eight visiting teams to a measly two goals between them – and even they were consolation efforts in the throes of a heavy defeat. The second statistic was perhaps less relevant, but to deeply superstitious football fans (probably the majority) no less important. Tottenham had only gained one victory at Hillsborough in 50 years, and that was way back in 1937. This combined threat was enough to send Bill Nicholson up to Sheffield a week early to cast his eye over Wednesday's game with the touring Soviets of Dynamo Tbilisi, who were also due to meet Spurs shortly. Nicholson watched the Yorkshire side stroll to a 5-0 victory and on the way back to London pondered how his side could break down that gritty Yorkshire defence. One thing was certain, if his players couldn't find a way through, then nobody could.

The usual Tottenham eleven set about the task of dismantling the Owls' impressive rearguard, but it remained unbreached when, midway through the first half, Smith let fly with a volley that had 'goal' written all over it. Even though Wednesday were fielding their reserve goalkeeper, McClaren was good enough to make an acrobatic tip-over that any goalkeeper would be proud to add to his collection.

Wednesday took the lead just before half-time, but that merely tweaked the Cockerel's tail and provoked an instant response from Norman, who added his name to the short list of Robson (Burnley) and Wagstaff (Manchester City) who had scored at Hillsborough this season. The visitors tried every trick in the book to search for the winner, but their attacks were rebuffed each time. Then Sheffield scrambled in a goal to make it 2-1. Nicholson's army promptly degenerated from a tightly disciplined force into an ill-organised rabble as they saw that their proud records of ten successive away wins since 15th April and eighteen unbeaten League games about to fall. Frustrated by their efforts to find a legitimate way past the Owls, they resorted to unbecoming tactics that veered from clumsy to downright dirty. Dyson illustrated this when he chased a hopeful ball into the penalty area and knocked goalkeeper McClaren senseless. In those days, of course, booking were rare, and sending offs so uncommon that players virtually had to be found guilty of attempted murder in order to be dismissed.

Tottenham's first defeat brought renewed hope, not only to Sheffield Wednesday and the other teams clinging in their wake, but to the neutral football fans who didn't want to see the championship remain a one-horse race. If the Owls could win their game in hand it would whittle Spurs' lead down to three points.

Two days after Tottenham's first defeat their fans enjoyed a bit of escapism when Dynamo Tbilisi descended on White Hart Lane. For a while it had been expected that Moscow Dynamo would be the tourists, but instead it transpired that the team from Georgia would appear in their place. Even though the match came swiftly after the disappointment of Tottenham's first defeat, Nicholson surprisingly fielded the entire first team, with the exception of Medwin, who replaced Jones. Tottenham looked ill at ease in the first half and Tbilisi were able to equalise Medwin's goal just before the break, before Mackay made it 2-1. After the interval Spurs stepped into their usual rhythm and the tourists were unable to keep pace. Mackay and Medwin both doubled their goalscoring tallies and White added a fifth, before Tbilisi reduced the arrears to 5-2. A crowd of 40,000 witnessed the fun, though a brief flaring of bad tempers towards the end reminded everyone that these Cold War adversaries were not to be trifled with.

As a rule of thumb, it's not good to visit a top side that's just been beaten, and this maxim was validated when Birmingham City visited White Hart Lane on 19th November. Spurs had something to prove and they soared into a 3-0 lead after only eighteen minutes. Seemingly embarrassed, they then took it easy for the next hour, but seeing that City were unable to make inroads they raised themselves to score another three towards the end.

The most curious feature of the game came when Allen of Birmingham brought down Allen of Spurs to concede a penalty with the score at 4-0. Skipper Blanchflower could have elected to take it himself like he usually did, but he didn't. He could have handed the ball to Dyson in order for the little dynamo to complete his hat-trick, but he didn't do that either. Instead he placed the ball on the spot and invited Bobby Smith to break his barren spell of four goalless games, which he duly did. This showed Blanchflower to be a master of psychological profiling, realising that his striking colleague was starting to lose confidence – fatal for a forward. As it was, the 6-0 outcome proved that not even a defeat by their closest rivals was going to throw Spurs off course. They wanted that title and nobody was going to stop them.

It wasn't only the first team which notched up a big score that day. Tottenham's reserves won 5-1 at Nottingham Forest, the 'A' team 4-0 at Newmarket Town, and the Juniors enjoyed a storming 8-1 victory at Crystal Palace, made even more remarkable by the fact that both Junior teams had gone into the game having won all their matches in the South East Counties League.

On the Monday, a curious exercise occurred at Tottenham's Cheshunt training ground, when Spurs played a 40-minute game against England, who were warming up for a midweek Home International Championship match against Wales at Wembley. Despite fielding four reserves, Spurs posted a 4-2 win, with a hat-trick from Dyson. England's two efforts had a Spurs connection, too. Jimmy Greaves got one, whilst Tottenham's reserve winger John Smith gave himself something to talk about for the rest of his life by grabbing the other. He was a temporary replacement for a late-arriving Bobby Charlton. Incidentally, Bobby Smith was destined to score in the international against Wales – to raise his England goals tally to six in four games – because he had grabbed a brace against Spain the previous month. Medwin and Jones featured in the Welsh side that collapsed 1-5.

Question: What does a manager do when his team aren't scoring many goals? Answer: He converts his full-backs into strikers. Well, that's what West Brom's manager Gordon Clark did as his team took the field at the Hawthorns to face Spurs. The experiment worked, too, because Don Howe and Williams proved reasonably effective, and Howe even managed a goal. Sadly for them, Spurs were already 3-0 up at the time, thanks to a brace from the rejuvenated Smith and one from Les Allen.

The draw for the third round of the FA Cup was always an eagerly awaited event, but especially so, now that Spurs looked set to land the Championship. Monday's lunchtime draw gave them a home tie against Second Division Charlton, which satisfied Bill Nicholson, and the bookies, who installed them as 13:2 favourites to land the Cup and achieve that ever-elusive double. The Cup-tie was still over a month away though, and attention was instead focused on the home game against the defending League Champions Burnley, who were lying fifth in the table. Burnley were struggling for good results at Turf Moor, but on their travels they feared no one. Nicholson hoped that Burnley would be tired from their midweek European Cup-tie at Stade de Rheims in France, which they lost 2-3, but went through 4-3 on aggregate.

It seemed as though their European adventure had drained the defending champions, because midway through the first half Tottenham hit them with their newly-acquired trick of scoring three goals in quick succession. It was hard on Burnley, who had matched Spurs all the way, made crueller when Mackay made it 4-0 with a 30-yard belter, though Burnley did pull back what seemed little more than a consolation just before the break. Spurs strode out onto the pitch in the second half confident that the points were in the bag.

It wasn't really complacency that led to Spurs' undoing, more a combination of determined players wearing claret and blue and some uncharacteristic goofs from Tottenham's normally reliable defence. Neither side were helped by the typical December weather of swirling wind and driving rain, which had helped to turn White Hart Lane into its usual gloopy mudbath consistency. Though Spurs tried their damnedest, they were unable to prevent Burnley from scoring the three goals that deservedly came their way. The 4-4 draw was certainly entertaining for the neutrals, but the weather had played its part. Nicholson explained that White Hart Lane was a peculiar ground to play on when it was windy, because both sides could be simultaneously running into a headwind, even when they were going in opposite directions. Also, you could stand in one spot and feel no wind, but move slightly and you could be in the teeth of a gale. Not that he was using that as an excuse, because it was equally problematic for both sides. He also reassured supporters that the pitch was still firm under the initial layer of mud, thanks to that plastic sheeting mentioned earlier.

It was just as well that half-time had provoked endless talking points amongst spectators, because Tottenham's matchday programme wasn't designed to provide ten minutes' worth of reading. Priced at twopence (just under a penny in today's decimal money) it consisted of four pages. The programme for reserve games was even poorer value for money, because you only got half the amount of writing, but were charged the same price for the privilege. Tottenham's secretary explained the anomaly by stating that whereas for a first-team game the club could make money on the programme because they'd sell 30,000 copies, they lost money on the reserve-team effort because they'd only sell 3,000. It didn't seem to occur to him that perhaps the first-team's programme could perhaps be improved to match the best efforts of other clubs. The only plus point to the programme was that it was free of the numerous adverts that plagued other club's offerings.

Tottenham faced three Lancashire sides in succession that December. On 10th they travelled up to Preston, but without their leading scorer

Smith, who was absent with a throat infection. Once again Frank Saul was drafted in as his replacement. Although Preston were fighting for their First Division lives, they put up an impressive show against what on paper were overwhelming odds. In the end, Spurs triumphed because they were slightly better than Preston in all departments, not vastly better. The solitary goal came from a corner-kick and was another training ground move. Maurice Norman launched himself above everyone and nodded the ball down to John White, who found space to pop the ball in. If the score was disappointing for the Preston board, they must have winced as they glanced around the empty terraces at Deepdale. Although it was traditionally a time when half-hearted footballing husbands were dragged round doing the Christmas shopping, Preston's accountants must have hoped that the visit of the League leaders would encourage a higher turnout. As it was, the attendance was a disappointing 21,657, the lowest First Division crowd to see a Spurs game that season, and the ground was only half full as a consequence.

If the first team struggled to find the net that day, the reserves showed them the way as they crushed Ipswich's second string 9-1. Six different players shared the goals, including both full-backs – Ken Barton and Mel Hopkins.

Tottenham's first-team squad jaunted off to Brighton on the Monday for a three-day break. This was now a traditional mini-holiday for the team to prepare them for the ardours of the hectic Christmas fixtures, and they indulged in some light jogging and rather more golf. Then it was time to head back up to Lancashire, to visit Everton, currently lying second, and one of the few teams with a slim chance of snatching away the championship. Everton were another example of a side that was prepared to buy success. Their latest acquisition was Alex Young, who had set them back £40,000. His signature brought their spending to £215,000, which was virtually the same amount Spurs had spent assembling their entire side. Even with Christmas just eight days away, there was no shortage of interest and over 61,000 braved the freezing fog to see the fun. Everton had yet to slip up at home, whilst Spurs had only succumbed once away from home. It promised to be a cracker.

The Toffeemen were lifted by a passionate crowd and controlled the game for half an hour on the treacherously slippery surface. They had left their shooting boots in the dressing room, however, and this proved to be their undoing. Tottenham had calmly soaked up the attacks, now they struck twice like a cobra sinking its fangs into a mesmerised victim. Messrs White and Allen injected the poison into the Goodison wound and made it a happy half-time dressing room. Everton's manager, Johnny

Carey, lifted the spirits of his dejected players for the second half, because they quickly pulled a goal back, but Mackay settled the destination of the points by smashing a 35-yard drive past goalkeeper Dunlop's ear. The only thing that threatened Tottenham now was the fog, which thickened noticeably at the end, causing the spectators behind the goals to lose sight of much of the action. Thankfully for Spurs, the referee did not abandon the game. The 3-1 win over the second-placed team gave Tottenham a massive ten-point lead over their closest rivals at the end of the day's play on 17th December. The season was just over half-completed.

	P	W	D	L	F	A	Pts
SPURS	22	19	2	1	71	26	40
Everton	22	13	4	5	55	36	30
Wolves	22	13	4	5	55	45	30
Burnley	21	14	1	6	63	39	29
Sheffield Wed	21	12	5	4	39	26	29

In case you're wondering where Everton's bitterest rivals Liverpool were, the answer is in the Second Division!

Tottenham's two Christmas fixtures were against fast-improving West Ham, who had racked up ten goals in two games, one of them an improbable 5-5 draw at Newcastle. Architect of their renaissance was an ex-Spurs player, David Dunmore, who had been a bit-part player for Tottenham for most of the 1950s. Round one of the double-header came on Christmas Eve, which was a Saturday. White Hart Lane hosted this fixture, and both sides looked as though they had over-indulged on the Christmas spirit the night before, because it lacked any edge. A fit-again Bobby Smith turned goal-provider with a couple of crosses that were headed in by White and Dyson, but otherwise Spurs were workmanlike, not wonderful.

The most entertaining moment came when Bill Brown sliced a goal-kick, David Dunmore instantly volleyed the ball back, only for Brown to redeem himself by finger-tipping the ball over the bar. Brown was one of two players who gave Nicholson his first injury crisis of the season when he received a leg injury against the Hammers. The other crocked player was Cliff Jones, whose longstanding knee injury returned to haunt him. Actually, crisis is too dramatic a word. Medwin was a ready-made replacement for Jones, whilst John Hollowbread was arguably the finest reserve keeper in the country, and had been first choice before Brown's arrival.

The Boxing Day return at Upton Park was a better game, though both of Spurs' opening goals were decidedly scrappy. Smith once again proved that he was happy to share the goals around, earning an assist for the third goal by steering a pass in the direction of John White. Hollowbread had a competent game at the other end and kept a clean sheet.

Tottenham celebrated their runaway lead with their traditional Christmas luncheon party, highlighted by the giving of Christmas gifts. Chairman Bearman was embarrassed (I presume) to receive an unedited copy of the year's most sensational book, *Lady Chatterley's Lover*, whilst tiny Terry Dyson was presented with a volume that the club thought he deserved – *Little Women*. Bobby Smith was given a model of a petrol filling station, because of his naughty habit of borrowing his teammates' cars and 'forgetting' to fill them up with petrol afterwards. Though a sense of humour was evident in the gift-giving, some of the players were miffed that the club weren't a little more generous in their choice of presents. After all, the maximum wage still precluded anything like a lucrative income. Top footballers in 1960 were not rich.

The New Year's Eve's game gave the 48,000 crowd inside White Hart Lane some anxious moments, as Blackburn were all-square, 1-1, at the interval. With an interesting team that included the youthful coupling of Derek Dougan and Peter Dobing, Rovers looked capable of inflicting on Tottenham their first home defeat of the season. That threat was blasted away in the second half as Spurs rattled up four goals in a devastating ten-minute blitz. The match ended 5-2 and was particularly enjoyed by Tony Marchi, given a rare game in place of the absent Mackay.

7th January 1961 was an eagerly awaited date in the football calendar, because it was the day of the third round of the FA Cup. Even though the Championship was starting to take on greater significance in the minds of supporters, it was still the Cup that occupied their hearts. Twelve months previously Spurs fans had also talked about the double as their team lead the First Division by three points, but the season had fizzled out with a League slide and a fifth-round Cup defeat at Blackburn. This time, whilst the title was looking more secure, comfort was gained in the significance of the figure '1'. With Cup wins in 1901 and 1921, and a championship in 1951, could 1961 provide similar blessings?

The visitors to White Hart Lane that day were Charlton Athletic, a middling Second Division side. Most pundits had written off the contest as a comfortable home win and were speculating about how big Spurs' winning margin would be. When Tottenham led 2-0 and then 3-1, their confidence seemed justified, but the Valiants lived up to their nickname by scoring again and threatening a dramatic equaliser.

Shock of the day came when Crewe Alexandra embarrassed Chelsea by winning 2-1 at Stamford Bridge. Crewe's manager Jimmy McGuigan declared he wanted Spurs in the fourth round, because his team was still smarting from the 2-13 fourth round replay drubbing inflicted by Spurs the previous season. He got his wish, though perhaps he would have preferred a Gresty Road clash, instead of a return to the Lane.

On Saturday, 14th January, Tottenham's first team were at Manchester United. For the loyal Spurs fans who travelled to the away games it was a long-awaited fixture. A total of 450 fans climbed aboard the 'Football Special', a train chartered from British Railways. Another hundred opted for the cheaper option of going up on one of the two coaches, but they had to leave Tottenham at 11pm on the Friday for the arduously slow journey up-country, with no motorways or bypasses to ease their journey.

Meanwhile a couple of hundred Irishmen sailed from Belfast to see their hero Danny Blanchflower in action. All these efforts were for nothing, for the game fell victim to a pea-souper fog. Whilst the train travellers and partying Irishmen had relatively straightforward journeys home, the poor so-and-so's who had come by coach found themselves stranded until the fog lifted slightly at 2.30am on Sunday morning. They finally made it back home in time for a late Sunday lunch, only to find the game had been rearranged for Monday night. It's not recorded how many of those weary heroes were up to another long haul back up to Manchester the following day.

The United game gave Nicholson his first genuine selection problems of the season. With Jones and Medwin both injured, John Smith, who made his first appearance since his debut the previous season, occupied the right-wing berth. Another injury victim was the unsung hero Peter Baker, who vacated his right-back position for the first time in nearly a year. He incurred his injury when sitting down on a chair, an action that burst a blood vessel behind his knee. Ken Barton, a Welshman who had been on Spurs' books for seven years without getting a sniff at first-team action, took Baker's place.

It would be easy to blame Tottenham's 0-2 defeat that night on these enforced changes, but that would be doing the Red Devils an injustice. They, too, had problems and goalkeeper Harry Gregg spent the second half as a striker after being clobbered by an over-enthusiastic Bobby Smith. United's No 9, Dawson, took over as an emergency goalie, and he played his part in keeping Tottenham goalless for the first time that season. If Dawson proved to be a useful keeper, then Gregg could have made a second career as a striker, because he craftily backheeled a ball into the path of Mark Pearson who rounded off the scoring at 2-0.

There were 65,295 inside Old Trafford that night, and there were only 44 fewer inside White Hart Lane for the derby fixture with Arsenal the following Saturday. Arsenal were a classic 'Jekyll and Hyde' team of the period, which can be gauged by two of their recent home games. They had been thrashed 2-5 by Burnley, then on the Saturday they had sneaked through 5-4 against Manchester City. Worryingly for the Gunners, they had to face a fully-fit Spurs that featured the same eleven that had kicked off the season back in August. Arsenal had a weakened side, but shocked Spurs by taking an eighth-minute lead. Alan Young meted out some tough tackling on Bobby Smith, leaving him hobbling, but was still unable to prevent Smith tapping in the third Spurs goal that clinched the game just before half-time. Also earning reprobation from referee Arthur Ellis was the hot-blooded Tommy Docherty, who offered a few choice words to the official to earn a booking. The 4-2 win gave Spurs the satisfaction of 'doubling' their rivals for the first time since 1955-56. Incidentally, fifteen locked-out supporters were able to break in by knocking at a gate, waiting for the steward to open it (he thought it was a policeman) and then rushing in.

Bobby Smith shook off his niggling injury for the Crewe Cup-tie, but took longer to shake off his embarrassment after being featured in a tabloid, being kissed. It wasn't some gorgeous model planting a smacker on Bobby's cheek that made him see red, but little Terry Dyson, who got carried away with a goal celebration. Crewe were in the top half of the Fourth Division and their players were determined to give Spurs a run for their money. Allegedly some of them earned themselves a few bob by unloading some of their personal allocation of 25 tickets to waiting ticket touts. Spurs surprised nobody by scoring three times in the opening 32 minutes, but Crewe had already scored a goal themselves by then, and superb goalkeeping by Brian Williamson shut Spurs out for the next half hour. Eventually, Tottenham won 5-1 to earn themselves a tricky fifth round tie at Villa Park, to be played a week after their League fixture in the same stadium.

A home game against Leicester would not normally be regarded as much of a problem, but the Foxes were enjoying their best ever season in the top flight since their heyday in the late 1920s. In addition, it had been a shock 1-2 home defeat by Leicester almost a year earlier which had sent Spurs spiralling out of championship contention. It was a case of history repeating itself when Spurs found themselves behind three times to an extremely committed East Midlands side. Two of Leicester's goals stemmed from some uncharacteristic hesitancy in the home defence, partially caused by a succession of long balls and fast running that seemed to catch them cold. When Spurs pulled it back to 2-2, through a penalty after Bobby Smith had been shoved in the box, Leicester permitted some roughness to creep into their play as a result of their outrage at the decision. The home fans hoped Spurs could capitalise on this indiscipline, but City regained their composure to score the winning goal with Norman at fault. Apart from the defenders, other players blamed for the defeat were John White and Bobby Smith, who were both subdued. Tottenham's first home defeat since 18th April 1960 (0-1 v Chelsea) wasn't too costly, because second-placed Wolves also lost, so the gap was maintained at eight points. Burnley and Everton had both hit a bad patch, so Spurs now only had two realistic challengers.

	P	W	D	L	F	A	Pts
SPURS	28	23	2	3	87	35	48
Wolves	28	18	4	6	62	53	40
Sheffield Wed	27	15	8	4	55	31	38

11th February saw the first part of the double header at Villa Park, which might determine whether Spurs could still become the first side to achieve the double since Aston Villa in 1897. Defeat in the League game might give renewed hope to Wolves, who were next in line to face Spurs. Aston Villa's game plan was to use inside-left Bobby Thomson to mark Blanchflower out of the action. The Tottenham captain had rightly been identified by Villa manager Joe Mercer as the most influential member of the team, and taking him out of the game seemed their best chance of victory. Villa knew him from the past, of course, because they had sold him to Spurs in 1954, possibly the worst bit of business they ever did. Blanchflower had won the Footballer of the Year award in 1957-58 and had also established himself as captain of Northern Ireland. He was starting a second career in journalism, and that month was selected to be one of Eamonn Andrew's victims for the TV show 'This Is Your Life'. Much to the embarrassment of the BBC (which carried the show live), when Andrews produced the famous red book and delivered the line – 'and tonight, Danny Blanchflower, this is your life' – Blanchflower promptly replied 'No it's not', turned his back and walked away. His refusal to participate meant a wasted journey for the Spurs team and his many family members and friends who were waiting for him in the studio. Quite why his family thought that this intensely private man would subject himself to so much personal publicity is not known.

At Villa Park, Bobby Thomson attached himself to Blanchflower like a limpet for 90 minutes, taking the opportunity to inflict some tasty tackles whenever possible, but the plan wasn't successful for two reasons. Firstly, Blanchflower was canny enough to anticipate the movements of teammates, so he was able to lay the ball off before Thomson could intervene; and secondly because Spurs had ten other master brains who could adapt to any situation, noticeably Mackay, who everybody wanted around them in an emergency. Villa held Spurs at bay throughout the first half, but were undone within 30 seconds of the turnaround when Smith headed in Allen's cross. Dyson soon made it 2-0, but Villa halved the deficit through a controversial penalty when Thomson was adjudged to have been pulled back by Henry. To most eyes it looked six of one and half a dozen of the other. By the close, Spurs had 50 points under their belts. No other First Division club in history had ever reached that milestone from only 29 games played.

If there was any doubt as to whether the average football supporter of the time preferred Cup to League football, it was removed by a glance at the attendance figures for the two Villa games. For the League match, 50,810 were inside the ground, whilst the Cup-tie a week later saw 69,000 descend on Villa Park. Villa were the undisputed Cup kings with seven trophies to their name, but only one of these had been in the last 40 years. Manager Joe Mercer now had to find a Plan B, now that Plan A had been so ruthlessly rubbished the week before. As the match started it was pretty nigh impossible to work out what that plan might be, as Spurs were busy dictating events. The tie was seen to be heading Tottenham's way after eighteen minutes, when swift interplay down the left resulted in a typically teasing cross from Les Allen. Jones stuck out a boot, full-back Neal stuck out a boot, and the ball struck both on its way into the net. Poor Villa were deflated and fell further behind when Smith created a bit of magic to start a move that was once more finished by Jones. Villa's determination to hit back in the second half was nullified by a cool, controlled Spurs defence. A frustrated Peter McParland was booked for treading on Mackay's hand. So Spurs took another stride closer to the double, and were drawn away at Sunderland in the quarter-final.

Had they not been involved in the Cup-tie at Villa Park, Tottenham would have been playing a League game at home to their closest challengers, Wolves. Instead, the game was rearranged for the following Wednesday, provided there was no replay. Curiously, Spurs also somehow persuaded Wolves and the footballing authorities to agree to postpone their Wednesday date if they had lost to Villa. The match would go ahead only if Spurs won. Quite why Wolves agreed to this isn't known, but surely they would have wanted to take on a dejected Spurs side straightaway? Anyway, the situation didn't arise and on 22nd February the top two clashed in front of 62,261 inside White Hart Lane, the biggest home gate of the season, apart from the local derby game with Arsenal.

As is so often the case when two titans clash, they cancelled each other out, in a 1-1 draw, with Smith scoring his 23rd League goal of the season so far. It was a good result for Spurs, as it kept the gap at a healthy eight points, with Sheffield Wednesday a further point behind, albeit with a game in hand. Spurs had maintained this safety margin since the beginning of December.

A visit to Maine Road now beckoned. Once again a Manchester curse seemed to strike, and Nicholson had a couple of changes to make in his otherwise settled side. Jones was absent once more, this time with a septic throat, and nobody was surprised when his ready-made replacement, Medwin, took his shirt. The other absentee was Norman (groin strain), who thereby missed his first game of the season. Tony Marchi yet again proved his versatility by stepping into his boots. Marchi had played in most of the defensive and midfield positions in his time with Spurs.

Manchester lived up to its wet reputation and the game was played in atrocious conditions of driving rain that turned the centre section of the pitch into a swamp. Most of the play was channelled out to the wings, where Spurs were strong (but where weren't they?). It may be reckoned that Tottenham's slick-passing may have foundered on mud heaps, but actually the players found it easier, because they didn't have to bring the ball under control, they could let the mud do that for them. An accurate long pass was virtually guaranteed to stay near a player's foot instead of running out of play or to an opponent. City were further handicapped by having an injured Joe Hayes stuck out on the wing for all the second half, and it was from there that Blanchflower crossed for Medwin to head the only goal. The 1-0 victory was made all the sweeter because Wolves lost at Cardiff, to leave Sheffield Wednesday as the only realistic challengers.

Chapter 8

~ ACHIEVING THE DOUBLE ~
(March-May 1961)

Nicholson was absent from the 1-0 win at Maine Road (assistant Harry Evans was in charge), preferring to take in Sunderland's 4-2 win at Leeds in a Second Division clash. He discovered the Rokerites were lethal at sticking away the few chances they created, but that their young side easily got disheartened when the going got tough. The importance Nicholson put on the FA Cup quarter-final at Roker Park is self-evident, and the Tottenham fans were keen too, because 10,000 made the long trip, although 6,000 tickets were hastily returned to Sunderland to meet the home club's demand. In the end, 63,000 were inside Roker Park, and most of them went deathly quiet when Spurs took the lead following a ninth-minute corner. If Nicholson's theory was correct, Sunderland's heads would drop, and Spurs could slow the tempo and hold them at bay, like they had done with the Villa.

For the remainder of the first half the plan worked well, though Spurs spurned several chances to kill the game. But early in the second half the tide turned. McPheat slammed the ball into the net and the famous Roker Roar was unleashed on the Londoners. To add to their discomfort the crowd invaded the pitch and suddenly the eleven men in white shirts must have felt very lonely. When order was eventually restored it was a backs against the wall job to fend off the resurgent red and white hordes. Sadly for Sunderland there was no team in the country better able to fulfil that role, with Norman and Mackay standing firm like twin lighthouses in a stormy sea and Blanchflower directing operations from his midfield command post.

The sanctuary of the dressing room was reached at 4.45pm and Spurs flew back to London on a chartered aircraft. A clue as to the estimated value of the Spurs team came with the insurance valuation for the flight that stood at a whopping £600,000. The team arrived back in London at 7.30pm and awaited the second instalment on Wednesday, 8th March.

Just under 65,000 pushed and jostled their way into White Hart Lane for the replay, causing fears of a possible tragedy. The turnstiles opened at 5.15pm at a time when fans were piling towards the ground having just left work. It is estimated that 50,000 arrived between 5.30pm and 6pm, which caused some minor crushing, as those at the back of the crowd were unaware of the hold-up at the front. It is a reminder that a tragedy like that at Hillsborough in 1989 could well have occurred at many football grounds in the 1950s and '60s. There was also congestion in the fixture lists because Tottenham's scheduled League match with Nottingham Forest had to be postponed.

Fans who could stretch their minds back to 1950 could remember the last time Spurs and Sunderland had met in the Cup at the Lane. On that occasion it was Sunderland who were the aristocrats and Tottenham the Second Division upstarts. In one of their most memorable afternoons, Spurs had come back from conceding the first goal to rip the 'Bank of England' side to shreds 5-1. Nicholson certainly remembered it, because he was playing that day, and it seemed as though it had permeated permanently into the minds of all 22 players on the pitch, because a similar result ensued this day. Deprived of the boost from the Roker Roar, the Sunderland players were exposed as young men playing a man's game. Spurs were at their peak as they cut the Second Division side down to size. There was no doubt that the Cockerels were ruling the roost in this tie. Five goals were scored without reply, including two for Dyson and one for Mackay.

No doubt Spurs were keen to draw the remaining Second Division survivors, Sheffield United, in the semi-finals, but instead they got Burnley, lying fourth in the First Division, but seventeen points behind Spurs. The good news for superstitious fans was that the match was to take place at Villa Park, where Spurs had already triumphed twice in the past month. That was also the bad news, because those with longer memories could recall three heartbreaking semi-final defeats at Villa Park against Blackpool (1948 and 1953) and Manchester City (1956).

Back in the League, a week before the semi-final showdown, Spurs had to visit Cardiff. The Welshmen were having a good season, though were unable to win any silverware (even the Welsh Cup proved to be beyond them). They did show resolve to take down the arrogant English team though, and Spurs found themselves quickly pegged back after taking an early lead. It got even worse when Tottenham regained that lead, because Cardiff struck twice in a minute to go ahead 3-2, their third goal coming from a jubilant ex-Gunner Tapscott. The Welsh side then shut up shop and defied Spurs to break down their steely defence. They couldn't. It was Tottenham's fourth League defeat of the season.

If another 32 people had squeezed into Villa Park on 18th March then it would have been a 70,000 crowd. Tottenham had prepared well for the game, staying in Wales for some rest and recuperation, not to mention light training on the Mumbles beach. They returned to London on the Wednesday to watch an England Under-23 game (colleague Frank Saul was a reserve), training hard on the Thursday, then travelling to the Midlands on the Friday. Poor Burnley had a tougher time. They had fielded what was tantamount to a reserve side against Chelsea on the Saturday, because in midweek they won 3-1 at SV Hamburg in the quarter-final first leg of the European Cup. Tottenham couldn't underestimate a side that they had failed to beat even when four goals up earlier in the season. Meanwhile, the vacant White Hart Lane ground hosted a Plymouth v Ipswich game in the Second Division, because Home Park was temporarily closed. This caused some grumbles among the Spurs groundstaff who had expected the afternoon off. Why White Hart Lane was picked is a mystery, though Ipswich must have been grateful to have saved themselves a long trek to Devon.

It seemed as though Burnley manager Harry Potts had hypnotised his players in the dressing room into thinking that they were once more four goals down, because they started the game at a furious pace, rocking a lethargic Spurs side on their heels. Once again Tottenham relied on their solid white wall to repel the invaders. On the rare occasions when the wall was breached, there was Bill Brown to mop up any remaining danger. It is doubtful whether Tottenham had withstood such an unremitting half-hour barrage all season, but at least they kept it goalless. Then came glorious relief as Spurs broke quickly to score the opener. Allen created the opening by flicking the ball towards Smith, who raced onto the ball, paused briefly, and then let rip with a fearsome drive.

Burnley held on without further damage until half-time, then endured agonies early in the second half when Robson had a goal ruled out for climbing over Norman, and then a penalty appeal turned down for an alleged handball by Henry on the line. Burnley's worst fears were realised when Spurs promptly scored from their next assault, and once again it was Smith who wielded the dagger. Burnley threw everything into attack as they attempted a rescue mission, but a minute from time Dyson made it 3-0. Though Spurs had not played particularly well, they had stood firm and done what was necessary to get through. Poor Burnley were left with nothing and not long afterwards exited the European Cup after a disastrous 1-4 defeat at Turf Moor in the second leg against Hamburg. Tottenham now had to banish all thoughts of the FA Cup final and concentrate on the League, because this time last season they blew a three-point lead and ended up marooned in third place behind Burnley and Wolves. Tottenham's fixture pile-up had now made things much tighter at the top:

	P	W	D	L	F	A	Pts
SPURS	32	25	3	4	93	40	53
Sheffield Wed	33	20	9	4	63	34	49
Wolves	35	21	6	8	89	65	48

The first of Tottenham's rearranged League games was at home to Newcastle the following Wednesday. The received footballing wisdom was that it was a good time to play a team distracted by an approaching Cup final, and the old theory was proved correct as a disjointed and jittery home side succumbed 1-2 to the Geordies. It was Spurs' second successive League defeat, they had used up their game in hand over the Owls, and now there were only nine games remaining. Were Spurs about to blow the League once again? At least they had a better-looking run-in than their Yorkshire opponents, and the two teams had yet to meet at White Hart Lane.

One of the easier-looking fixtures was away to Fulham, though the Cottagers had decided now was the time to put on a spurt to ease their relegation worries. To aid their cause they had acquired centre-half Bill Dodgin from Arsenal, and he needed no encouragement to slow down Tottenham's relentless march to the title. Deadlock at both ends was the outcome, though the absence of Mackay and Smith were crucial factors. Previously, only Manchester United had managed to keep Spurs from scoring, and supporters had to reach back in their memories to August 1959 to remember their team's last goalless draw. Worse news accompanied Sheffield Wednesday's win. The gap was down to three points with eight games to play.

The fixture committee had given Spurs home games on Good Friday and Easter Saturday, followed by the short trip to Chelsea on Easter Monday. A huge 65,000 crowd besieged White Hart Lane on Good Friday for the first game with Chelsea, swelled by casual supporters hoping to make the Cup final. The club had announced that all season ticket holders would be guaranteed a Wembley ticket (though not necessarily a seat) whilst the remaining tickets would be issued on a lucky dip basis. Vouchers would be distributed at an undetermined home game and could be handed back to the club by supporters, keeping their fingers crossed that they would be one of the lucky 5,000 or so to be pulled out of the hat. The identity of match that would feature these vouchers was kept secret, in order to frustrate ticket touts and no doubt ensure healthy gates at all home games until the vouchers appeared.

No voucher appeared at the Chelsea game and for 49 minutes there weren't any goals either. Frank Saul was having no more luck in front of goal than anyone else, and the fans bemoaned the absence of the injured Smith. It seemed as though the frustrations of the home crowd had built to bursting point, but Cliff Jones then smashed the ball into the net from an Allen pass to release the tension. Poor Chelsea were overwhelmed as Spurs players queued up to stick the knife in. Three more goals followed, but the game had a farcical conclusion. Henry and Norman collided, not once, but twice, to gift Chelsea two goals in the closing moments. The final score was 4-2.

The magic vouchers appeared on Saturday, but for some reason only 41,000 home fans collected them, so the odds of winning a ticket were about 8:1. One person who definitely did not enjoy any luck was bottom-club Preston's goalkeeper Kelly, who watched in horror as White's hopeful punt bounced out of his hands and trickled over the line after only four minutes. White had suffered a goal-drought for three months, so he was eternally grateful for the fluke, whilst Kelly (normally Preston's reserve keeper) probably put it down to April Fool's Day. Cliff Jones was certainly not fooling. He rattled up a brilliant hat-trick, displaying three different goalscoring skills in the process. First he showed his dribbling prowess, beating a couple of defenders to notch up League goal number 100 for the season. Then he displayed his poaching abilities by stealing the ball virtually out of the keeper's hands for his second, before sealing his perfect day with a spectacular overhead kick. Also enjoying a happy afternoon's work was Frank Saul, who scored his second goal in two days.

The short hop to Chelsea on Easter Monday attracted a crowd of 57,000 and they were rewarded by one of the most entertaining games of the season, even if the bulk of the crowd were disappointed by the result. The popularity of watching Spurs at this time can be gauged by the fact that only 20,000 were at Highbury to see a mediocre Arsenal side take on Fulham.

By the time the half-time interval came round at Stamford Bridge, the neutrals in the crowd would have doubted whether there was going to be that much to cheer them in the second half. The fates seemed to have conspired against the Pensioners in the opening half. Firstly the returning Bobby Smith had headed Spurs in front after only seven minutes, and then Jimmy Greaves thought he'd equalised, only for a linesman to rule offside. Greaves gave the referee his considered opinion on the decision, and his ill-chosen words earned him a booking. The final nail in the coffin was an injury to Chelsea's Brabrook after 34 minutes that reduced the Blues to ten men. The only possible hope for the home fans was the way in which Chelsea had kept Spurs on their toes, and the fact that Peter 'The Cat' Bonetti had kept the score down to 0-1.

Early in the second half Chelsea received three gifts from the hand of fate, which cancelled out their earlier woes. Firstly Blunstone smashed in an equaliser; then Mackay suffered an injury that left him a passenger for the rest of the match; finally a Greaves goal was declared legitimate. Chelsea were now 2-1 ahead and a weaker side than Tottenham might have capsized, but if you're going to win the title, you have to have the mental strength to recover from adversity. Medwin made it 2-2 by running on to Smith's bouncing through ball, and then Norman added a third by heading in Mackay's free-kick. Obviously, Mackay's injury did not prevent him striking dead-balls!

So it was a perfect Easter. Spurs were the only team in all four divisions to record three wins and the aggregate score was 12-4. Their nearest challengers, Sheffield Wednesday, had dropped two points, widening the gap to five, whilst Wolves' slim chances had evaporated with two defeats out of three. They were now nine points adrift and had played a game more. All Spurs had to do now was to pick up six points from their remaining five games to clinch the title. Perhaps not even that, because the showdown with Wednesday was only two matches away.

Psychologically it would have been easy for the Spurs players to ease up slightly, with the championship seemingly won. That they did not is down to a combination of a steely manager and a competitive bunch of players. They might have had the occasional off day, but they always gave it everything they had. In the away game at St Andrew's they raced into a 3-0 lead after only 32 minutes. It was almost as if they were planning to go in at half-time and offer a ceasefire to save the Brummies from further suffering. City weren't prepared to let go that easily, and pulled one back from the penalty spot after a stray leg had brought down Jimmy Bloomfield in the box. Not long after half-time it was 2-3, when Harris netted again, this time from open play. With 40,000 screaming fans roaring the Blues on, it was another stiff mental examination for the Whites. They passed it once again by sticking to what they did best – keeping possession with slick passing and intelligent running, which kept the pressure off the overworked defence. If the Chelsea game had shown they had the nous to come from behind, this game demonstrated that Tottenham knew how to defend a lead under pressure. They had passed almost all the qualifications needed to be declared worthy champions.

Sheffield Wednesday had drawn that day, so the title race was a race no longer. To cause the upset of the century, Wednesday needed to give Spurs a thumping in the next game on Monday, 17th April, then hope that Spurs got thrashed in their last three games, whilst the Owls notched up three further big wins.

Achieving the Double *(March-May 1961)*

	P	W	D	L	F	A	Pts
SPURS	38	29	4	5	109	48	62
Sheffield Wed	38	22	12	4	73	39	56

Evening games at White Hart Lane usually kicked off at 7.30pm, but for the crucial clash with Sheffield Wednesday it was put back to 8pm. This was nothing to do with the demands of television (you would be fortunate to catch a glimpse of Tottenham anywhere on the box in that era, two full seasons before Match Of The Day). No, it was police advice that necessitated the delay. Fearful of another bout of gridlock in north London, they wanted to give the rush hour traffic an extra half-hour to disperse before the football traffic hit the streets *en masse*. The club acceded to their request.

Although their hopes of snatching the championship were only likely to come true in the pages of boys' fiction, Sheffield Wednesday weren't going to let Tottenham take it easy. The Yorkshire side had already been shell-shocked when manager Harry Catterick departed to join Everton; they didn't want to lose anything else. Both teams threw themselves into the fray with gusto and cancelled one another out until the Owls took the lead after 28 minutes. Mackay, never a shrinking violet, went in hard against Fantham, but illegally and on the edge of the box, too. Fantham dusted himself down and slammed his free-kick into the white and blue wall, whereupon the ball spun kindly into the path of Megson, who blasted it home.

Wednesday's lead lasted less than fifteen minutes, before a quick double strike from the home team on the verge of half-time left them reeling. First, Smith barged his way into the penalty area to slam in the leveller, and then before the roars had died down, Spurs showed their dead-ball skills. Blanchflower floated over a free-kick that Norman nodded into the path of Allen, who did the rest.

The second half continued in rumbustious vein. Both Mackay and his opponent, Johnson, found themselves in the referee's notebook for tackles that made hard men wince, and near the end Smith barged into goalkeeper Ron Springett in classic centre-forward mode, sandwiching the hapless goalkeeper between a rock (Smith) and a hard place (the post). Springett somehow regained consciousness within five minutes and gamely carried on. Finally the whistle went, confirming that Spurs were Champions of England, although the trophy would not be presented until their final home game, against West Brom, in twelve days time.

The last three League games were now an anticlimax, but Nicholson urged his men on by reminding them they were still playing for their Cup final places. The other carrot he dangled before them was the opportunity to establish the biggest points total in one season. The record of 66 had been achieved by Arsenal exactly 30 years before, and Tottenham only needed to pick up three points from those last three games to overtake their neighbours.

Fittingly, the last away League game was at Turf Moor, the home of the previous champions, Burnley. Sportingly the Burnley players formed two lines and applauded the new title-holders onto the pitch. Burnley then contrived to lose two goals through defensive blunders, before proving that last December's astonishing four-goal comeback was no fluke. Inspired by Jimmy McIlroy, they managed the seemingly impossible feat of making Tottenham look bad, as they scored a quartet of goals to win the game 4-2. The biggest surprise was the realisation that such a fine side were languishing in fifth place, seventeen points behind Tottenham at the end of the day.

Only two home games to go, and a Wednesday night fixture against Nottingham Forest was a meaningless affair, with only 35,743 bothering to show up, Tottenham's lowest crowd of the season. Medwin scored the only goal of the game, whilst Marchi stood in once more for the absent Mackay. There were 16,000 extra souls inside the stadium for the final game, against West Brom, as the Championship trophy was officially presented, though Spurs had already been given the trophy beforehand. The crowd were also hoping for at least a draw, which would carry Spurs above the high water mark of 66 points. It wasn't to be. Although Smith equalised for Spurs early in the second half, his side seemed to be preoccupied with the Cup final and didn't deserve to draw. The lively Baggies had struck the woodwork three times, so nobody could complain when Robson struck the winning goal on 74 minutes. This meant Spurs had to share Arsenal's record haul of 66 points, a total that would be overhauled by Leeds (67 points in 1968-69) and Liverpool (68 in 1978-79), before the three points for a win system was introduced in 1981.

Tottenham did, however, set a number of new Football League records that season. Their sixteen away wins constituted a new best, as did their total number of 31 League victories. They also had that eleven-match winning start. A couple of other records were equalled. Their haul of 33 away points was level with Arsenal again, whilst only Manchester United (1956-57) and Wolves (1958-59) had beaten as many as eleven clubs home and away in the League. No side had scored more than Tottenham's 115 League goals since Arsenal in 1932-33, and no side has come close to that figure since. Although that prolific marksmanship is a tribute to Spurs' brilliance, it was a freakish season for goalscoring, with the champions of all four divisions hitting a century of League goals. Needless to say, that had never happened before, nor since.

Tottenham only had a week to psyche themselves up for the Cup final. On the Friday night they trooped to the cinema to see 'The Guns of Navarone'. The FA Cup and League Championship double had only been achieved twice, by Preston (1888-89) and Aston Villa (1896-97). Throughout the twentieth century it had become a seasonal talking point as time and time again teams failed in their bid to emulate them. Some pundits seriously speculated that it was an impossible feat, even though a few teams had come very close. Manchester City (1903-04), Aston Villa (1912-13), Manchester United (1947-48) and Wolverhampton (1959-60) had all won the Cup whilst finishing second in the League. Ironically, it was Spurs who had scuppered Wolves' League title bid by winning 3-1 at Molineux in their penultimate League game. Three teams had secured the League title, but lost the Cup final, and remarkably it was Villa who won the Cup on all three occasions. Clearly, Villa didn't want to lose the distinction of being the last club to claim the double. The unlucky Cup losers were Newcastle (1904-05), Sunderland (1912-13) and Manchester United (1956-57).

One important note should be made about Preston and Villa's doubles. Preston only had to survive a 22-game League season and five Cup-ties. Villa's was barely any tougher, with a 30-game League campaign and five rounds of the Cup. Tottenham, however, had to triumph over a 42-game League slog and then win six FA Cup rounds in succession (with one replay) if they were to land their double.

Tottenham's Wembley opponents, Leicester, had finished sixth in Division One. Whilst Spurs had only happy memories of finals (they won in 1901 and 1921), Leicester had only known pain, when losing 1-3 to Wolves in 1949. Tottenham's victories had been gained at Crystal Palace and Stamford Bridge in the pre-Wembley era, so watching their team at Wembley was a novel experience for Spurs fans. Most of the players had experience of Wembley's unique aura at international matches and the like, so it wasn't a novelty for all of them.

Leicester's side did not contain many household names at the time, and to younger fans nowadays only two names stand out. Gordon Banks had already established himself as England's Under-23 goalkeeper, but would not oust Sheffield Wednesday's Ron Springett from the full England side for another two years. Right-half Frank McLintock would become an integral part of the Arsenal side which also achieved the double in 1970-71. Otherwise, the Foxes were reckoned to be a collection of unexceptional players, fashioned into a useful team by the shrewd boss

Matt Gillies. Leicester also had injury worries. Jimmy Walsh and Ken Keyworth survived late fitness tests, whilst Tottenham were at full strength with their favoured line-up that had kicked off the League season back in August.

Whilst Leicester had rested key players in their last League game (even goalkeeper Banks), Tottenham kept the same eleven that played the previous Saturday. Although Wembley's long, springy turf was always found to be tiring – and Henry, Blanchflower, White, and Allen had yet to miss a competitive fixture – Spurs hoped to overcome the fatigue factor by steering passes to feet and reducing the amount of running required. They aimed to call upon their incredible fitness levels, attributable to the pioneering training work done by Bill Watson, not to mention the day-to-day training overseen by unsung hero Cecil Poynton. The one player who was doubtful for the game was Bobby Smith, who was still troubled by a leg injury. He needed pain-killing injections, which would, it was hoped, see him through the game.

Although Leicester were one of the few teams to have beaten Spurs this season, the thick mud of winter was felt to have been a crucial factor in that game, and Tottenham's slick-passing style was reckoned to be more likely to succeed at Wembley than Leicester's more-rugged running game. After the first nineteen minutes there was no way of telling if this was going to be the case. Tottenham had created the best chance, when White blasted over the bar, but the Foxes were stringing together some good moves themselves. It was honours even.

Then the infamous Wembley jinx struck again. Seven out of the past nine FA Cup finals had been blighted by a crippling injury to a player. The most famous examples are Bolton's Eric Bell pulling a muscle in the 'Matthews final' of 1953 and the broken neck sustained by Bert Trautmann of Manchester City in 1956. The two most recent finals had seen broken legs for Roy Dwight (Nottingham Forest, 1959) and Dave Whelan (Blackburn, 1960). This time it was Leicester's right-back Len Chalmers who was singled out. He was reduced to being a passenger on the left wing following a tackle from Allen. Those critics who favoured the introduction of substitutes now had further evidence to support their case, but the twelfth man wasn't seen at the showcase event until 1967, when once again Tottenham were involved.

Whether or not the injury to Chalmers changed the result is a matter of conjecture. Spurs fans may point to a controversial offside decision against Cliff Jones as mitigation that they too suffered a dose of bad luck. Dodgy offside decisions had been a bone of contention all season. Tottenham players had made a habit of astute through balls to onrushing forwards, but innumerable judgments had gone against them. Nicholson reckoned that linesmen were too busy looking at the man with the ball, rather than the free player running on. Nicholson argued that in the split second between the linesman switching his eyes to the attacker, he had advanced that extra yard, and earned himself an unjust raised flag in the process.

This controversy might seem to take the gloss off Tottenham's victory, but it shouldn't. It was still an enthralling game whose result was in doubt until the 69th minute, when Spurs opened the scoring. Dyson aimed a cross at Bobby Smith and the fearsome striker smacked the ball past Banks. The boys in blue seemed to wilt after that, and it was no surprise when the same two Spurs players combined for the second. The only curiosity was that the roles were reversed – Dyson defying his lack of inches by launching to head in Smith's cross.

Finally, referee Jack Kelly put the whistle to his lips and proclaimed Tottenham Hotspur as the first team to win the double in the twentieth century. It sparked massed celebrations, and at times it seems as though they have never really ended. It was arguably the greatest club skipper of all time who fittingly stood on the famous steps and held the magnificent trophy aloft and brought tears to the eyes of the hardest Tottenham Teddy Boy. For Danny Blanchflower, it was the perfect culmination to the season, for he had already earned his second 'Footballer of the Year' award from the sportswriters (his first had been won in 1957-58).

A crowd of 250 players, wives, club officials and invited guests took part in the celebration banquet at the Savoy that evening, with Transport Minister Ernest Marples as guest of honour. Marples summed up the season by stating: 'It is not only what you have achieved, but also the manner in which you have achieved it. You have been showing us the arts and graces of the game, with a great deal of poise, balance and rhythm.' Nicholson in turn praised the Minister for the new electrified train service to White Hart Lane, and then turned his attention to the reserve team who 'did not win any honours, but have always been pulling their weight'. Nicholson also paid tribute to the 'A' team, who won their championship, and the youths, who had done likewise, but with the added bonus of not losing any of their seventeen games. The post-speech cabaret featured Harry Secombe and Roy Castle, followed by a presentation of a new recording by the 'Tottenhamites' entitled 'Tip Top Tottenham Hotspur', which may have to take the blame for pioneering an excruciating form of aural torture.

The following afternoon tens of thousands of well-wishers had their chance to pay their tributes as they lined the route of the open-topped double-decker bus procession from Edmonton Town Hall to Tottenham Town Hall. As the bus started out there were only a few souls milling around. Terry Dyson turned to Dave Mackay and voiced his fears that there was hardly anybody there and they were in for an embarrassing ride. It was only when the bus swung into the main road that Dyson's anxiousness evaporated. A vast crowd filled every vantage point and a huge wall of sound erupted around his ears. There was no escape from the cheers and waves and general hullabaloo on the three-mile journey, especially when the bus passed White Hart Lane. From the top of the bus the players waved the two precious trophies at the directors applauding from the boardroom windows. There was even more noise generated as the bus crawled past the Royal Dance Hall, as the resident band launched into the fans' favourite 'McNamara's Band'.

The jubilant players enjoyed a week's rest before undertaking a brief tour of Holland, where they beat Feyenoord 2-1 and an Amsterdam XI 3-0. It was a fitting reminder that after their well-deserved summer break they would be taking on the cream of the continent in the European Cup.

Chapter 9

~ How the Mighty Fell ~
(1961-77)

Everyone connected with Tottenham Hotspur from the Chairman down to the most casual supporter was confident that their club was destined to become the team of the 1960s, in much the same way that Arsenal had dominated the '30s. Having imposed themselves on both domestic competitions so convincingly, it was generally felt that there was no club that could realistically thwart their ambition of achieving a second successive championship. Wolves, Burnley and Sheffield Wednesday had been firmly put in their place, whilst 'sleeping giants' like Everton, Manchester United and Arsenal were probably going to slumber on quietly for the next season or two. The FA Cup was always a bit of a lottery – a tricky away tie or a poor performance could put paid to the ambition of retaining that particular trophy – but for once, the domestic Cup had to share top-billing with the novelty of competitive European football in the shape of the European Cup.

Player-wise, Bill Nicholson kept faith with the winning combination. There was no great urgency to replace anybody, and the quality of the players just outside of the first team had been self-evident when they had been called upon. The manager was concerned that excessive reliance was placed on the strong shoulders of barnstorming centre-forward Bobby Smith, and began delicate negotiations with AC Milan over the possibility of bringing back Jimmy Greaves, who had joined the Italian club from Chelsea in the summer. Though Spurs had a few fast, tricky players, none were out-and-out goalscorers like Greaves and none could hope to match the mastery that the little genius had displayed in his favoured role. Greaves had cracked in 124 goals for Chelsea in just 157 League games and his pedigree was not in question. It was apparent from those in the know that Greaves wasn't settling in easily in Italy, and Nicholson was hopeful he could prise him away. A forward line-up featuring the very different talents of Smith and Greaves, in tandem, would surely be a match for the very best that Europe could offer. As for English opponents, they wouldn't have a hope.

As the 1961-62 season kicked off, the signing of Greaves was nothing more than a pipe dream. After beating an FA XI 3-2 in the Charity

Shield at White Hart Lane, Spurs proceeded to lose three of their opening nine League games. This set the tone for the season. Quite why the champions should display bursts of inconsistency was down to a number of factors. For one, the side never had a settled look about it, with a number of injuries forcing changes, which gave Nicholson headaches as he sought to juggle tactics and positions. None of the ten players who had notched up at least 36 appearances the previous season was able to improve on that total. With a few gaps now appearing in what used to be a solid defensive wall, it was inevitable that the opposition gained renewed heart and felt able to take games to Spurs, instead of holding back and allowing themselves to be bounced upon. Perhaps a few Spurs players lost a little bit of confidence which affected their form, but whatever the cause, it meant that a dampening defeat was usually just around the corner, every time two or three victories had seemed to right the team's wrongs. The New Year was a particularly torrid time, with only one League victory in the first nine games of 1962.

By this time Greaves was on board, having been finally pinned down by Nicholson at the end of November for a record £99,999. The peculiar fee was down to Nicholson, who didn't want his new player to have the added pressure of being the world's first £100,000 footballer. That honour went to Alan Ball (Blackpool to Everton) five years later. Though Greaves settled in quickly, notching up 21 League goals in 22 appearances in that first season, it was more problematic for Nicholson to work out the best partner to have alongside him. Smith and Allen competed for this privilege, but it was usually the wandering wingman, Cliff Jones, who was number two behind Greaves in the goalscoring charts.

So Tottenham relinquished their title, but to whom? The answer was a club with a fascinating set of links to the 1951 Spurs side. Ipswich Town had only enjoyed one season in the Second Division in their history when Alf Ramsey took his first steps in League management. He steered his new charges to the Third Division (South) title in 1956-57, followed by three middling Second Division seasons. Using all the tactical nous he had learned over the years from such luminaries as Arthur Rowe, he added a few of his own to the mix and blended it into a side that captured the Second Division title in 1960-61. Most pundits predicted that keeping Town out of the relegation places would be success enough; nobody seriously expected them to be title contenders.

Just like the Tottenham side of which he'd been such an integral part, Ipswich hoodwinked the established sides by playing to a system no one else had fathomed or knew how to counter. Both sides had the advantage of bursting into the First Division, using the element of surprise to catch their opponents unawares. Ipswich's revolutionary tactics employed Jimmy Leadbetter as a joker in the pack. Although wearing a No 11 shirt, he eschewed the normal practices of a left-winger and kept a healthy distance from the opposing full-backs, sending a bewildering variety of balls up to Ted Phillips and Ray Crawford, uniquely operating as a pair of giant strikers. Even accomplished defenders like Maurice Norman found it impossible to stop two battering rams charging at them, and before long teams were forced to field two huge centre-halves to cope with them, or else draw the full-backs inside to provide safety in numbers.

Ipswich proved their worth by beating Tottenham home and away, though if Spurs had managed to stamp their authority on either of these games, then they would have retained the Championship, because the gap between the teams at the finish was only four points, with Burnley sandwiched in between. Ipswich's 56-point total would have only earned them fourth place in Tottenham's double season, but few begrudged them the Championship.

The pain of failure was even harder to bear, because Tottenham kept a tight hold of their other trophy in fine style, thus nearly allowing themselves the distinction of winning consecutive League and Cup doubles. In their seven Cup games, their free-scoring attack bagged 24 goals, despite being drawn away at Birmingham, Plymouth and West Brom in the first three rounds. Aston Villa found themselves beaten 0-2 once more, this time at White Hart Lane, and then Manchester United were disposed of 1-3 in the semi-final. Burnley provided the opponents at Wembley this time, and Tottenham had to play rather better than the previous season to overcome them, though the scoreline was still a convincing 3-1. Bobby Smith enjoyed the accolade of scoring in both finals. The Spurs line-up for the 1962 final was different from 1961 only in having Greaves and Medwin replace Allen and Dyson.

The big change to have taken place in the ten years that separated Spurs' title successes was the advent of organised European competition. Although Spurs had been playing top European outfits for 50 years (they toured Germany in 1911, for example), the European Cup would in time prove the ultimate prize. In its early years, this was far from the case. For one thing, there was the sheer novelty aspect of playing competitive football in far off lands against unknown teams in a two-legged system. Not to mention problems with visas, and such like. Tottenham's first European Cup preliminary round tie, at Gornik Zabrze behind the Iron Curtain in Poland, typified some of the problems. Spurs were overturned 2-4, but when they brought the Poles back to White Hart Lane, the home team turned the tables by the improbable margin of 8-1.

Tottenham marched onwards, overcoming Feyenoord of Holland 4-2 on aggregate, and then beating the Czech club Dukla Prague by the same margin, despite losing the away leg. This sent them through to a semi-final with defending European champions Benfica, who had replaced the previously imperious Real Madrid as the cream of Europe. Tottenham lost 1-3 in Portugal, victims of bad refereeing and poor defending, but almost turned it around at the Lane, winning 3-2 and hitting the woodwork three times as they pressed for the equaliser.

The following season, 1962-63, Spurs did taste European triumph, in the Cup-Winners' Cup final where they crushed Atletico Madrid 5-1 in Rotterdam. Nicholson had by now learned how to deal with the intricacies of Continental football, and earned his side the accolade of being the first from Britain to win a European trophy. Only Manchester United had previously threatened to find the key to unpicking the lock of foreign defences, which stubbornly proved to be superior to English ones, but they were still recovering from the tragedy at Munich. A representative side from London had reached the final of the Inter-City Fairs Cup in 1958, but they had lost, as did Birmingham City in 1960 and 1961. Rangers carried Scottish hopes in 1961, but they too fell at the final hurdle, this time in the Cup-Winners' Cup. It seemed as though British clubs were for ever going to be the poor relations of Continental competition.

Travelling large distances to unknown parts of the Continent, eating unfamiliar food in unfamiliar hotels, tested the expertise of many a British club secretary. Managers, coaches and trainers struggled to cope with opposition tactics that were, quite literally, foreign to them. Two-legged ties were an alien concept to teams used to gung-ho tactics in a one-off Cup-tie, and most of the British teams qualifying for Europe came unstuck when trying to impose their uncompromising style against teams equipped with more subtle arts. It is no coincidence that the managers who finally cracked the conundrum and grabbed the honours were the more intellectual kind, blessed with an ability to think outside the box, as modern parlance has it. Bill Nicholson led the way, followed by Ron Greenwood (West Ham, Cup-Winners' Cup 1965), Jock Stein (Celtic, European Cup 1967) and Matt Busby (Manchester United, European Cup 1968). Mention must also be made of Alf Ramsey, the only manager of England to collect a top prize. Once more the Tottenham connection was paramount. That Spurs style was a European one, not a domestic one, and could be adapted to suit whatever set of players one cared to pick for whatever team.

Tottenham themselves have never (yet) won the domestic League title again, although in 1962-63 they sometimes touched the heights of the double side with some breathtaking displays. Defending champions Ipswich were beaten 5-1 in the Charity Shield at Portman Road and were thrashed twice in the League for good measure. Nottingham Forest were humbled 9-2 at White Hart Lane, whilst Bill Shankly's Liverpool were toppled 7-2 at the same ground in mid-April. Nicholson's side had lost the necessary consistency though, and five days after thrashing Liverpool they lost 0-1 at Goodison Park to effectively allow Everton to take the title. Spurs' goal-haul that season was 111 in the League, with a record 37 coming from Jimmy Greaves.

In the next, 1963-64, season Tottenham and Greaves were again leading scorers, though the goals against figure of 81 tells the main story of why the double side was starting to fall apart. Bill Nicholson desperately sought to rebuild, as once formidable players slowly edged towards the twilights of their careers. Bill Shankly's Liverpool emerged from the shadows, whilst Don Revie's Leeds United burst from the Second Division to further shove a faltering Tottenham into the quieter waters towards mid-table.

The regulars in the double side stayed together until that 1963-64 season, and the first to go was Terry Medwin, who had effectively been first reserve in that great side as he battled to win a place against Terry Dyson. Ironically, Medwin had just started to win that battle with his arch rival, when he suffered a broken leg in a tour match. Barely into his 30s, he was forced to quit and went into coaching, most notably at Fulham. Like so many of his colleagues he had been taught well by Nicholson. He was able to pass on much of what he had learned as assistant manager to John Toshack, when Swansea broke into the top flight for the first time in the early 1980s. He is currently living in his native Wales.

The 1964-65 Tottenham side was bereft of three star players who had graced White Hart Lane with such outrageous success. The first to leave was Danny Blanchflower, who had disguised his age so well on the pitch that it came as a surprise to many that he was 38 years old. Such was his ability that he probably had the brains to carry on a bit longer, but unlike the other old-timer who bowed out around that time, he was burdened by crippling injuries. Blanchflower might have been a natural for management, but instead moved into journalism, where he became a stalwart of the *Daily Express*, thrilling millions with his outspoken opinions, tempered with the knowledge that he had the ability and experience to back them up. Blanchflower passed away in 1993 aged 67.

If Blanchflower's passing was felt to be premature, that was nothing to the grief that swept through the footballing world on 21st July 1964 when the death of John White was announced at the ridiculously tender age of 27. He had been playing golf in Enfield and taken shelter from a storm under an oak tree. A bolt of lightning took away this immense talent. Thereafter his nickname, 'The Ghost of White Hart Lane', acquired a more poignant slant, and throughout that 1964-65 season many fans stood waiting in vain for that elusive figure to magically pop up in front of goal like he'd done countless times before.

In 1964-65 Bobby Smith was still wearing white and blue, but now it was in the stripes of Fourth Division Brighton. Yorkshire grit had carried him through the pain of numerous injuries at Spurs, and when he could no longer ply his trade in the top flight he soldiered on at the Goldstone Ground, where his eighteen League goals helped Archie Macauley's side to the title, and repaid his £5,000 transfer fee ten times over. Smith then dropped down into non-league football. He is still living in London and was the subject of a recent biography.

By this time, Tottenham were merely one of many good teams, instead of the undisputed masters, as the Lancashire triumvirate of Everton, Liverpool and Manchester United took turns to capture the Championship. The first elements of Nicholson's rebuilding strategy were now in place, with Pat Jennings sharing the green jersey with Bill Brown, Phil Beal occasionally swapping duties with Mackay, Cyril Knowles filling in at right-back, before later taking Ron Henry's left-back berth, Alan Mullery stepping into the void left behind by Blanchflower, not to mention Alan Gilzean frightening defenders all over the country. All these players, plus a few more, were to form the backbone of the side which took Tottenham through the 1960s and into the brash '70s, but for a period in the mid-'60s there was an intriguing combination of newcomers mixing it alongside survivors from the double side.

The one exception was Tony Marchi, who could trace his ancestry back to the original push and run side, and was now playing a much bigger part than his earlier perpetual-reserve role. He was now playing in at least half of Spurs' matches, with a penchant for European games where he bolstered the back line as an extra defender. It was perhaps unfortunate that Marchi found himself competing for a place with the likes of Blanchflower, Mackay and Mullery. At another club with lesser talents to contend with, he may have been a famous figure in his own right. As it is, it's perhaps only Tottenham fans of the time who can appreciate his true worth to the side, and then perhaps, not all of them.

Marchi left in 1965 to become manager of Cambridge City, at the time one of the top sides in the Southern League. He then moved across to Northampton Town, temporarily arresting their spectacular slide from the First Division to the Fourth. He now resides in Essex.

How the Mighty Fell *(1961-77)*

In 1965-66, three more of the double side bowed out of White Hart Lane. Peter Baker was perhaps the least well-known, mostly because he filled the unglamorous right-back berth, and also because he went about his business in a competent, if unspectacular way. He was approaching his mid-30s when he made way for the brasher Cyril Knowles. Certainly it's hard to imagine Peter Baker inspiring a pop record (remember 'Nice One Cyril' by the Cockerel Chorus?). Perhaps on reflection, this is a compliment to Baker, not an insult. The stalwart defender emigrated to South Africa, fulfilling a player-manager role at Durban City.

Les Allen suffered from the 'Marchi syndrome', victim of a four-way split as three contenders all vied to take his position. It ranks as a tribute to Allen that he was able to hang on for so long, despite the competition from Jimmy Greaves, Bobby Smith and Alan Gilzean. Allen provided something that none of the others could, despite their knack for scoring goals. Allen's talent was an ability to go about his business, making goals for others, then appearing from nowhere and converting a chance for himself as opposition defenders grappled with those they regarded as the more-dangerous strikers.

Perhaps the only consolation for Les Allen was that he was still young enough (28) to ply his trade elsewhere. He joined unfashionable Queen's Park Rangers, then a long-established Third Division outfit, for £21,000. Allen helped lift Rangers into the First Division by the end of the 1960s, firstly as a player, then as a manager, earning himself a League Cup winners medal in 1967. He took charge of another renowned League Cup side, Swindon Town, in 1972 (replacing Dave Mackay), but that was a less successful posting and Swindon eventually slipped towards the Third Division. There was definitely a footballing gene unique to the Allen family though, because his son Clive and nephew Paul both ascended to the heights that Les had achieved. Les Allen now lives in Essex.

Terry Dyson was three years older than Allen, but in 1965 he was able to stay in the top flight by joining Fulham, even though they seemed destined – as ever – to plunge into the Second Division. Yet again they contrived a remarkable escape. In 1968 he dropped into the lower divisions with Colchester United, but retired at the age of 35 in 1970. He is now to be found in Middlesex.

By the time 1965-66 had run its course, Spurs were shovelled down to eighth place by the likes of Leicester and West Brom. European football was no longer a seasonal delight, their hold on the Cup-Winners' Cup having been snatched at Manchester United in December 1963.

Ron Henry survived into the 1966-67 season (just) before his knees gave out, but he had played in virtually all of the previous season's games in his left-back role. Totally committed and professional, he astonished everyone in 1965-66 by actually scoring a goal, his first in nearly 300 League games. Manchester United were the victims as he let rip from nearly 40 yards. Thereafter he soldiered on in the reserves, and continued to serve his beloved club by coaching younger players who were aspiring to reach the heights of their mentor. Henry is yet another ex-Spur to retire to within a short drive of White Hart Lane, namely Middlesex.

Maurice Norman was only three months older than Henry, and lasted a similar length of time, despite breaking his leg in November 1965 against a touring Hungarian side. Norman had the strength of a Shire horse and was able to make a brave comeback when most players would have called it a day, but he was never the same.

Finally we come to the goalkeeper, Bill Brown, who defied his age by regaining his place between the sticks, despite the attentions of an Irishman called Pat Jennings, who had obvious talent and who was fourteen years younger than Brown. After Jennings eventually took over, Brown played briefly for Northampton Town before emigrating to Canada and joining Toronto Falcons.

The two final members of that double side clung on tenaciously for a couple more seasons, thus earning themselves a third FA Cup winner's medal when they helped to overcome Chelsea 2-1 in 1967. Dave Mackay and Cliff Jones were the durable duo, though Jones only earned his medal by coming on as a substitute, whilst Mackay grabbed the glory of lifting the famous trophy aloft as club captain.

This was no more than Mackay deserved. In December 1963 he broke his leg in a European Cup-Winners' Cup-tie against Manchester United at Old Trafford. Nobody was really surprised that Mackay had the grit to come back from that, but when he broke that same left leg on his comeback nine months later, against Shrewsbury's reserves, everyone must have expected that it signalled the sad end to a great career.

Everyone except Dave, that is. Mackay fought his way back to fitness yet again by the start of the 1965-66 season, after an almost unprecedented twenty-month lay off. Even more amazingly, he barely missed a game for nearly three seasons, and even regained his place in the Scottish side for his 22nd and final cap in October 1965, alongside teammates Bill Brown and Alan Gilzean. Incidentally, Billy Bremner, who appears with Mackay in one of the classic photographic images of all time, took his place in the Scottish side. Such is the colossal image that envelops Mackay, it is something of a surprise to study the picture and realise that Mackay is hardly any taller than the diminutive Bremner. Mackay had a seven-foot heart within a 5ft 8in frame.

Mackay stepped down from his pedestal in 1968, fearful that his reputation may have been besmirched by merely ordinary performances as he hit his mid-30s. He needn't have worried. He played alongside Roy McFarland in Brian Clough's remarkable Derby side, though Mackay had departed by the time County collected their Championship trophy in 1971-72. Mackay bowed out at the top.

His managerial career looked as though it was destined to be less successful. Mackay had flings at Swindon (player-manager) and Nottingham Forest, before stepping into the shoes of Brian Clough – who had decamped for lowly Brighton – at Derby County. Nobody but Mackay could have predicted that he could rebuild the Rams and lead them to the Championship once more, but that is exactly what he did in 1974-75.

Mackay went on to manage Walsall, Doncaster, and Birmingham City, and had spells as a coach in Kuwait and Egypt as well. He is now retired and living in Nottinghamshire.

Tottenham enjoyed a prosperous season in 1966-67. Not only did they regain the FA Cup, but they also showed true Championship form for most of the campaign, only failing to emulate the achievements of '51 and '61 because of a wobbly autumn. They eventually finished four points adrift of Manchester United, and missed out on the runners-up spot to Nottingham Forest on goal-average.

The last survivor of the double side wore the white shirt of Spurs until October 1968, when he left for Fulham. Cliff Jones had demonstrated similar tenacity to Mackay in shaking off injuries, so it's fitting that these two players were the last to go. By now the Spurs line-up consisted of the new generation of players, including Joe Kinnear, Terry Venables and Martin Chivers. Although Tottenham never dominated the 1960s like they threatened to, they can bask in the knowledge that they were the top side of that decade, based on average League positions, ahead of Everton, Manchester United, and Burnley.

Bill Nicholson remained as Tottenham manager until 1974, an impressive reign of sixteen years that is twice the length of the next most successful Spurs boss – Keith Burkinshaw – was able to achieve. Nicholson kept Tottenham in the top half of the table towards the end of his career and though he could never quite recreate the magic of that double side, he nonetheless was able to step down with his remarkable managerial career untainted with the stigma of failure, which is unusual in the footballing world. (The four games lost at the start of 1974-75 which prompted his resignation, cannot be deemed a failure, as it is only a blip in a span of sixteen years). A campaign has been launched to persuade the powers-that-be to award Nicholson a knighthood. I don't know if there is a set of criteria that is used to decide on these things, but my theory is that two tests must be passed.

Firstly, a potential footballing knight must have achieved a remarkable level of success. No problem there, even Matt Busby could only equal Nicholson's haul of eight major trophies, and you could probably make out a convincing case simply on the grounds of winning the League and Cup double and masterminding the first British team to a European trophy. Then you have to add on his remarkable longevity, with regular additions of silverware along the way, and then cast your mind back to his marvellous playing career.

The second evaluation concerns the style with which this success was achieved. Bill Nicholson was a true gentleman, who won the respect of almost everyone he met during his long career. He was fair-minded, level-headed, even-tempered and surely possesses all the personal qualities needed to win his knighthood. Certainly, some less worthy individuals have been accorded the honour and it's about time he did.

Although devotees of Tottenham Hotspur are still awaiting (impatiently) another championship, over the years the club have added further trophies to their cabinet room. The first of these was the League Cup in 1970-71. Tottenham didn't enter that competition until 1966-67 – its seventh year. Many of the top teams had refused to enter, but gradually its worth increased. The prospect of a Wembley final may have provided the incentive to make Tottenham reconsider. Their triumph on 27th February 1971 saw new goalscoring sensation Martin Chivers net both goals in a 2-0 win over Aston Villa.

Finishing third in the League that season entitled Spurs to enter the UEFA Cup, which replaced the defunct Fairs Cup. Tottenham made it to the final, where they faced another English side, Wolves. Spurs squeaked through 3-2 on aggregate, earning Nicholson the honour of becoming the first English manager to capture two European trophies.

Tottenham won the League Cup again in 1972-73 with a 1-0 win over Norwich, but then came a long drought. By now, Tottenham were no longer challenging for the title or qualifying for Europe. Instead they were desperately trying to keep their heads above water. They narrowly avoided relegation in 1974-75, but finished bottom in 1976-77.

It is a sad fact that Spurs have seldom looked like scaling the heights. The advent of the Premier League in 1992-93 has done little to help matters. Not so long ago Tottenham considered themselves one of the Big Five English clubs. No longer. While they wait for the arrival of a new golden age, fans can console themselves with memories of those glorious two seasons when Tottenham Hotspur were Champions of England.

~ Guide to Seasonal Summaries ~

Col 1: Match number (for league fixtures); Round (for cup-ties).
e.g. 4R means 'Fourth round replay.'

Col 2: Date of the fixture and whether Home (H), Away (A), or Neutral (N).

Col 3: Opposition.

Col 4: Attendances. Home gates appear in roman; Away gates in *italics*.
Figures in **bold** indicate the largest and smallest gates, at home and away.
Average home and away attendances appear after the final league match.

Col 5: Respective league positions of Tottenham and opponents after the game.
Tottenham's position appears on the top line in roman.
Their opponents' position appears on the second line in *italics*.
For cup-ties, the division and position of opponents is provided.
e.g. 2:12 means the opposition are twelfth in Division 2.

Col 6: The top line shows the result: W(in), D(raw), or L(ose).
The second line shows Tottenham's cumulative points total.

Col 7: The match score, Tottenham's given first.
Scores in **bold** show Tottenham's biggest league win and heaviest defeat.

Col 8: The half-time score, Tottenham's given first.

Col 9: The top line shows Tottenham's scorers and times of goals in roman.
The second line shows opponents' scorers and times of goals in *italics*.
A 'p' after the time of a goal denotes a penalty; 'og' an own-goal.
The third line gives the name of the match referee.

Team line-ups: Tottenham line-ups appear on top line, irrespective of whether
they are home or away. Opposition teams are on the second line in *italics*.
Players of either side who are sent off are marked !
Tottenham players making their league debuts are displayed in **bold**.

LEAGUE DIVISION 1   Manager: Arthur Rowe   SEASON 1950-51

No	Date		Att	Pos	Pt	L	F-A	H-T	1	2	3	4	5	6	7	8	9	10	11
1	H 19/8	BLACKPOOL	64,978	16	7	L 0	1-4	0-2	Ditchburn Farm	Ramsey Shinwell	Withers Wright	Nicholson Johnston	Clarke Hayward	Burgess Kelly	Walters Matthews	Bennett McCall	Duquemin Mortensen	Baily Slater	Medley Wardle

Scorers, Times, and Referees: *Baily 65 [Kelly 77] Johnston 20, 89, Mortensen 32,* Ref: T Rand
It's Spurs' first top-division game for fifteen years. Stan Matthews dismantles the left side of Tottenham's defence, allowing three of Blackpool's goals to come from the advancing wing-backs. Baily's goal brings temporary hope, but that is soon snuffed out by the Seasiders.

| 2 | A 23/8 | BOLTON | 21,745 | 10 | 19 | W 2 | 4-1 | 1-1 | Ditchburn Hanson | Ramsey Roberts | Withers Banks R | Nicholson Barrass | Clarke Gillies | Burgess Howe | Walters McShane | Murphy Moir | Duquemin Lofthouse | Baily Bell | Medley Langton |

Scorers: *Murphy 37, Walters 60, Medley 66, Langton 35 [Duquemin 80]* Ref: G Tedds
Peter Murphy has been signed from Coventry and he takes Bennett's place today. He beats four men in a dazzling 35-yard run before scoring the equaliser. Any more 'delightful forward interchange' and Spurs will regain their nickname of 'The Wonder Team', speculates one reporter.

| 3 | A 26/8 | ARSENAL | 64,638 | 12 | 5 | D 3 | 2-2 | 1-1 | Ditchburn Swindin | Ramsey Barnes | Willis Smith | Nicholson Shaw | Clarke Compton L | Burgess Mercer | Walters Cox | Murphy Logie | Duquemin Goring | Baily Lishman | Medley Roper |

Scorers: *Burgess 22, Walters 70 Roper 17, Barnes 88p* Ref: E Baker
The last time the teams met at Highbury in Division One (October 1934), eventual champions Arsenal beat soon-to-be-relegated Spurs 5-1. This time there is no gap in ability and the Gunners are only saved when Lishman was needlessly brought down, resulting in the late penalty.

| 4 | H 28/8 | BOLTON | 44,246 | 4 | 18 | W 5 | 4-2 | 2-2 | Ditchburn Hanson | Ramsey Banks R | Willis Banks T | Nicholson Barrass | Clarke Gillies | Burgess Howe | Walters McShane | Bennett Moir | Duquemin Lofthouse | Baily Bell | Medley Langton |

Scorers: *Duquemin 35, 42, Howe 59 (og), Moir 11, 20 [Baily 75]* Ref: G Tedds
Twice Langton and Moir combine to deadly effect to put Spurs behind, but afterwards Bolton are thoroughly outplayed. Several scoring chances are spurned until Duquemin heads in Medley's cross. Despite the comfortable win, bad misses save the Trotters from a slaughtering.

| 5 | A 2/9 | CHARLTON | 61,480 | 9 | 4 | D 6 | 1-1 | 1-1 | Ditchburn Bartram | Ramsey Shreeve | Willis Lock | Nicholson Fenton | Clarke Phipps | Burgess Forbes | Walters Hurst | Bennett O'Linn | Duquemin Vaughan | Baily Cullum | Medley Duffy |

Scorers: *Ramsey 10p Vaughan 44* Ref: A Williams
Despite taking the advantage through Ramsey's penalty, once again Spurs are unable to take full advantage of their attacking edge, once the Valiants have equalised. Though Spurs' pretty approach play is much in evidence, it cannot penetrate Charlton's well-organised defence.

| 6 | A 6/9 | LIVERPOOL | 39,015 | 12 | 8 | L 6 | 1-2 | 0-2 | Ditchburn Sidlow | Ramsey Lambert | Willis Spicer | Nicholson Jones | Clarke Hughes | Burgess Paisley | Walters Payne | Murphy Taylor | Duquemin Stubbins | Baily Done | Medley Balmer |

Scorers: *Medley 48 Stubbins 6, Balmer 41* Ref: S Law
The legendary Albert Stubbins brilliantly steers in Payne's cross with his head to give Liverpool the lead, then Balmer pounces on a Willis miskick to make it 2-0. Medley cuts in and shoots from close range to reduce the deficit, but the home side retain their lead in the driving rain.

| 7 | H 9/9 | MANCHESTER U | 60,621 | 9 | 8 | W 8 | 1-0 | 1-0 | Ditchburn Allen | Ramsey Carey | Willis Aston | Nicholson Gibson | Clarke Chilton | Burgess Cockburn | Walters Bogan | Bennett Downey | Duquemin Rowley | Baily Pearson | Murphy McGlen |

Scorers: *Walters 45* Ref: T Glendenning
It's the same old story. Poor attacking play threatens more dropped points for the Spurs. Walters brings home the bacon though, when his shot nutmegs Aston and slips past unsighted goalie Allen. The improved defensive covering does ensure the first clean sheet of the season so far.

| 8 | A 16/9 | WOLVERHAMPTON | 55,364 | 12 | 5 | L 8 | 1-2 | 0-1 | Ditchburn Williams | Ramsey McLean | Willis Shorthouse | Nicholson Crook | Clarke Chatham | Burgess Wright | Walters Hancocks | Bennett Dunn | Duquemin Swinbourne | Baily Pye | Medley Mullen |

Scorers: *Chatham 69 (og) Swinbourne 3, Hancocks 55* Ref: A Ellis
A great end-to-end thriller, but lively Wolves are keen to test the mightily impressive Ditchburn at every opportunity, whilst once again Spurs are bereft of ideas up front. Assistant manager Jim Anderson hints that a visit to the transfer market may have to be made before very long.

| 9 | H 23/9 | SUNDERLAND | 59,190 | 13 | 19 | D 9 | 1-1 | 1-0 | Ditchburn Mapson | Ramsey Stelling | Willis Hedley | Nicholson Watson | Clarke Walsh | Burgess Wright A | Walters Wright T | Uphill Broadis | McClennan Davis | Baily Shackleton | Medley Reynolds |

Scorers: *Baily 33 Broadis 57* Ref: A Denham
Uphill and McClennan are brought in to try to rejuvenate the Spurs attack, but McClennan lasts only 20 minutes before an accidental collision means a month's stay in hospital for a gashed chin. Inevitably, ten-man Spurs can't hang on to their lead and former player Ivor Broadis levels.

| 10 | A 30/9 | ASTON VILLA | 36,538 | 9 | 18 | W 11 | 3-2 | 1-1 | Ditchburn Hindle | Ramsey Parkes | Willis Dorsett | Nicholson Powell | Clarke Martin | Burgess Moss F | Walters Craddock | Murphy Gibson | Duquemin Ford | Baily Thompson | Walters Smith L |

Scorers: *Murphy 37, Medley 56, Duquemin 68 Thompson 32, Smith 48* Ref: B Griffiths
Murphy equalises from 25 yards from his temporary left-half position and then a well-organised Tottenham grind out a much-needed win.

148

#	Date	H/A	Opponent	Attendance	Result	Scorers	Team (positions 1-11)	Referee	Match Report
11	7/10	H	BURNLEY	46,518	W 1-0	Medley 49	Ditchburn, Tickridge, Willis, Nicholson, Clarke, Brittan, Walters, Murphy, Duquemin, Bennett, Medley / Strong, Hayes, Mather, Rudman, Woodruff, Bray, Stephenson, Morris, Holden, Potts, Chew	Ref: J Topliss	Baily and Ramsey are on international duty and Burgess is injured, but their replacements all play well. It's still the attack which is hindering Spurs' championship ambitions and only Medley deserves any credit. He deservedly gets the winner when he neatly tucks away a Walters cross.
12	14/10	A	CHELSEA	65,992	W 2-0	Walters 55, Duquemin 58	Ditchburn, Ramsey, Willis, Nicholson, Clarke, Brittan, Walters, Bennett, Duquemin, Bennett, Medley / Medhurst, Bathgate, Williams, Armstrong, Harris, Mitchell, Campbell, Bowie, Bentley, Billington, Gray	Ref: W Everett	Lowly Chelsea gamely hold on for nearly an hour, but then a defensive blunder allows Walters to score. Medley then crosses for the 'Duke' to head home and an easy win ensues. Bennett is having a poor run and is being regularly criticised. He has had a transfer request turned down.
13	21/10	H	STOKE	54,124	W 6-1	Duquemin 10, 22, Walters 29, Ormston 68 [Ben't 55, 89, Med' 85]	Ditchburn, Ramsey, Willis, Nicholson, Clarke, Brittan, Walters, Bennett, Duquemin, Bennett, Medley / Herod, Mould, McCue, Sellars, Mountford, Kirton, Ormston, Bowyer, Brown, Johnston, Oscroft	Ref: Rev S Davis	Three straight wins seem to have given confidence to the jittery Lilywhites attack and Stoke pay the price. Bennett nets twice, but Walters scores the best goal after racing 30 yards to head home Willis's free kick. It should have been seven, but Ramsey unusually misses a penalty.
14	28/10	A	WEST BROM	44,543	W 2-1	Walters 12, Medley 32 Barlow 88	Ditchburn, Ramsey, Willis, Nicholson, Clarke, Brittan, Walters, Bennett, Duquemin, Bennett, Medley / Sanders, Rickaby, Millard, Kennedy, Vernon, Barlow, Elliott, Williams, Richardson, Betteridge, Allen	Ref: R Burgess	A reprise of the clever free-kick from the last game allows Spurs to take the lead against the run of play. They then dazzle the Throstles with a vintage demonstration of the 'push and run' game. Baily's trickery sets up Medley for the second, but WBA's goal is no more than a token.
15	4/11	H	PORTSMOUTH	66,402	W 5-1	Duquemin 22, Walters 24, Willis 42 (og) [Baily 47, 49, 80]	Ditchburn, Ramsey, Willis, Nicholson, Clarke, Brittan, Walters, Bennett, Duquemin, Bennett, Medley / Butler, Earl, Ferrier, Scoular, Spencer, Dickinson, Harris, Reid, Clarke, Ryder, Froggatt	Ref: E Vickery	Portsmouth have won the championship for the past two seasons, but they are a shadow of their former selves. Three key injuries further undermine them and Spurs take full advantage with a scintillating display. Baily deserves his hat-trick for his superb showings this season.
16	11/11	A	EVERTON	47,125	W 2-1	Baily 24, Medley 61 Buckle 51	Ditchburn, Ramsey, Willis, Nicholson, Clarke, Brittan, Walters, Bennett, Duquemin, Bennett, Medley / Burnett, Clinton, Moore, Grant, Jones, Farrell, Buckle, Fielding, McIntosh, Potts, Eglington	Ref: R Leafe	Tottenham prove their championship credentials by passing the traditional test. They grind out a win, despite playing well-below par against the bottom side. Ditchburn forms a green wall and on the occasions that it is breached there is usually a defender available to clear off the line.
17	18/11	H	NEWCASTLE	70,336	W 7-0	Bennett 5, Baily 22, Medley 30, 63, 70 [Walters 52, Ramsey 74p]	Ditchburn, Ramsey, Willis, Nicholson, Clarke, Brittan, Walters, Bennett, Duquemin, Bennett, Medley / Fairbrother, Cowell, McMichael, Harvey, Brennan, Crowe, Walker, Taylor, Milburn, Robledo G, Mitchell	Ref: W Evans	In the most devastating display of 'push and run', the Geordies' strong defence is shredded by a bewitching combination of short passing and intelligent running. A crowd of over 70,000 crams into White Hart Lane to see the thrills. The record gate is 75,038 versus Sunderland in 1938.
18	25/11	A	HUDDERSFIELD	39,519	L 2-3	Nicholson 51, Walters 54 Glazzard 16, Hassall 32, Metcalfe 49	Ditchburn, Ramsey, Willis, Nicholson, Clarke, Brittan, Walters, Bennett, Duquemin, Bennett, Medley / Wheeler, Gallogly, Kelly, Battye, McEvoy, Boot, McKenna, Nightingale, Glazzard, Hassall, Metcalfe	Ref: G Tedds	Huddersfield haven't won in five, but they show tremendous finishing to go three goals clear early in the second half. In a thrilling game Spurs come back strongly, but the Terriers hold on gamely. Bill Nicholson is philosophical. The winning run had to end somewhere down the line.
19	2/12	H	MIDDLESBROUGH	61,148	D 3-3	Ramsey 14p, Duquemin 20, Mannion 17, Medley 70 (og)	Ditchburn, Ramsey, Willis, Nicholson, Clarke, Brittan, Walters, Bennett, Duquemin, Bennett, Medley / Ugolini, Robinson, Dicks, Bell, Whitaker, Gordon, Delapenha, Mannion, Spuhler, McCrae, Hartnett	Ref: F Thurman	With magical Wilf Mannion in their side, Boro play a game one not dissimilar to Spurs, but with more long balls to the wings. This pays dividends on a heavy pitch and Spurs have to equalise three times to earn a point, the last one coming from a disputed corner. Poor finishing costs a win.
20	9/12	A	SHEFFIELD WED	44,367	D 1-1	Bennett 43 McJarrow 40	Ditchburn, Ramsey, Willis, Nicholson, Clarke, Brittan, Walters, Bennett, Duquemin, Bennett, Medley / Morton, Bannister, Curtis, Gannon, Packard, Witcomb, Rickett, Henry, McJarrow, Froggatt, Woodhead	Ref: W Ling	Ramsey blasts a penalty over the bar after 14 minutes and the early-season lack of confidence seems to have returned on a ground where Spurs have won once in 40 years. At least they equalise when Medley's teasing cross soars over the goalkeeper giving Bennett a very easy header.
21	16/12	A	BLACKPOOL	22,203	W 1-0	Duquemin 75	Ditchburn, Ramsey, Willis, Nicholson, Clarke, Brittan, Walters, Bennett, Duquemin, Bennett, Medley / Farm, Shimwell, Garrett, Johnston, Hayward, Kelly, Matthews, Mudie, Mortensen, Withers, Perry	Ref: T Rand	Blackpool are handicapped by an injury to Hayward, the effective shackling of Stanley Matthews by Nicholson and Willis, and a snowy pitch which seems to hamper them more than it does Spurs. The winner comes when Medley whips in a low cross that is met by the diving 'Duke'.

LEAGUE DIVISION 1   Manager: Arthur Rowe   SEASON 1950-51

No	Date			Att	Pos	Pt	F-A	H-T	Scorers, Times, and Referees	1	2	3	4	5	6	7	8	9	10	11
22	23/12	H	ARSENAL	54,898	3	W	1-0	1-0	Baily 41 Ref: E Baker	Ditchburn Swindin	Ramsey Scott	Willis Barnes	Nicholson Forbes	Clarke Compton L	Burgess Mercer	Walters McPherson	Bennett Logie	Duquemin Goring	Baily Lishman	Medley Cox
					2	31			The clash of the titans is long-awaited and there were inaccurate rumours that this game was going to be switched to Wembley. In the event, 20,000 fewer than expected turn up and they miss a vintage battle. Arsenal's form is shaky and Spurs now appear ready to take over at the top.											
23	25/12	A	DERBY	32,301	2	D	1-1	1-1	Murphy 27 McLaren 38 Ref: W Everett	Ditchburn Brown	Ramsey Mozley	Willis Parr	Nicholson Ward	Clarke Oliver	Burgess Musson	Walters Harrison	Bennett Stamps	Duquemin Lee	Murphy Morris	Medley McLaren
					10	32			Burgess and Baily are injured, so Murphy and Brittan miss out on their Christmas lunch. Murphy's consolation is a goal to earn a point. Both sides have goals ruled out. Duquemin's effort is chalked off for a foul, whilst Lee's early header is adjudged not to have quite crossed the line.											
24	26/12	H	DERBY	59,885	2	W	2-1	1-0	McClennan 20, 50 McLaren 51 Ref: W Everett	Ditchburn Brown	Ramsey Mozley	Willis Parr	Nicholson Ward	Clarke Oliver	Burgess Musson	Scarth Harrison	Murphy Stamps	McClennan Lee	Baily Morris	Medley McLaren
					11	34			McClennan fills the boots of the injured 'Duke' with aplomb. His second goal is a beauty. He mesmerises Musson and Mozley then steers past Brown and taps into an empty net. The other emergency forwards aren't as good, and Scarth misses some tempting chances to bag a hat-trick.											
25	30/12	H	CHARLTON	54,667	1	W	1-0	1-0	Walters 35 Ref: A Williams	Ditchburn Bartram	Ramsey Revell	Willis Lock	Nicholson Fenton	Clarke Phipps	Burgess Forbes	Walters Hurst	Bennett Lumley T	Duquemin Vaughan	Baily Evans	Medley Kiernan
					19	36			Prime Minister Attlee watches Spurs go to the top of Division One for the first time since 1933. Their 1-0 win on the frozen pitch enables them to move ahead of Middlesbrough thanks to a goal average that is 0.73 better. Arsenal are third – they've lost three out of their last four games.											
26	13/1	A	MANCHESTER U	45,104	1	L	1-2	1-1	Baily 7 Rowley 15, 48 Ref: T Glendenning	Ditchburn Allen	Ramsey Carey	Willis Redman	Brittan Gibson	Clarke Chilton	Nicholson Cockburn	Walters Birkett	Murphy Aston	McClennan Pearson	Baily Rowley	Medley Rowley
					9	36			A classic encounter between two of the great entertainers in League football. The Red Devils come back from behind to keep the points but the result is in doubt until the final whistle. Strangely, Spurs extend their lead at the top on goal-average because Arsenal beat Middlesbrough 3-1.											
27	20/1	H	WOLVERHAMPTON	66,796	1	W	2-1	1-0	McClennan 31, Walters 55 Walker 60 Ref: A Ellis	Ditchburn Williams	Ramsey Short	Willis Pritchard	Brittan Crook	Clarke Shorthouse	Burgess Wright	Walters Hancocks	Murphy Walker	McClennan Swinbourne	Baily Dunn	Medley Mullen
					5	38			Another feast is served up for a bumper crowd as two teams on top form slug it out. Spurs win through better finishing. Eleven of Tottenham's remaining 15 games are against bottom-half opposition and Arthur Rowe is confident that the championship is on its way to White Hart Lane.											
28	3/2	A	SUNDERLAND	56,817	1	D	0-0	0-0	 Ref: A Denham	Ditchburn Mapson	Ramsey Hedley	Willis Hudgell	Nicholson McLain	Clarke Walsh	Burgess Wright A	Walters Wright T	Murphy Davis	McClennan Ford	Baily Shackleton	Medley Duns
					15	39			(a much more modest signing from Lovell's Athletic) keeps him quiet. It's definitely a day for the defences as Spurs go a point clear at the top. Since September's meeting Sunderland have splashed out £30,000 on Trevor Ford to form the bedrock of their 'Bank of England' team. Clarke											
29	17/2	H	ASTON VILLA	47,842	1	W	3-2	1-0	Baily 20, Medley 46, Ramsey 80p Dixon 65, Gibson 75 Ref: B Griffiths	Ditchburn Rutherford	Ramsey Parkes	Willis Lynn	Brittan Canning	Clarke Martin	Burgess Moss F	Walters Dixon	Murphy Thompson	McClennan Jeffries	Baily Dorsett	Medley Gibson
					21	41			Spurs take the lead through a 25-yard Baily blockbuster. Medley's goal makes it 2-0, but Villa soon level. Then controversy after Ramsey was upended in the box. Rutherford saves Ramsey's initial spot-kick, but he moves early and the ref orders a retake, which Ramsey duly converts.											
30	24/2	A	BURNLEY	33,047	1	L	0-2	0-1	Chew 26, 49p Ref: J Topliss	Ditchburn Strong	Ramsey Woodruff	Willis Mather	Nicholson Adamson	Clarke Cummings	Burgess Bray	Walters Chew	Murphy Morris	McClennan Holden	Baily McIlroy	Medley Lyons
					9	41			Spurs players find Chew's two goals difficult to digest. They claim Ditchburn was clattered by Holden, allowing Chew a free header for the first and they say Clarke's handball was accidental. Some Spurs fans want Duquemin back in the attack. He scores a hat-trick for the reserves.											
31	3/3	H	CHELSEA	59,449	1	W	2-1	2-0	Wright 5, Burgess 20 Campbell 75 Ref: R Burgess	Ditchburn Medhurst	Ramsey Winter	Willis Hughes	Nicholson Williams	Clarke Harris	Burgess Mitchell	Walters Hinshelwood	Murphy Armstrong	Wright Bentley	Baily Dickson	Medley Campbell
					20	43			Wright justifies his surprise selection by scoring within five minutes of his debut. A second goal after 20 minutes kills the game and Spurs go to sleep against a poor Chelsea side. A pigeon landing on top of a goal provides the most entertainment after that for the 60,000 dozing crowd.											

150

#					Score	Att											
32	A	STOKE	10/3		1-0 D 0-0 0-0	24,236 11 44	Ditchburn Wilkinson	Ramsey Watkin	Willis McCue	Nicholson Sellars	Clarke Mountford	Burgess Kirton	Walters Siddall	Murphy Bowyer	Wright Mullard	Baily Johnston	Medley Ormston

Ref: Rev S Davis
Spurs draw another blank, but they remain three points clear at the top. Because Middlesbrough also draw, Newcastle are threatening a late charge on the rails, so the goal-drought must be sorted out pronto. Luckily Mullard was as wasteful in front of goal as the Spurs' strikers were.

| 33 | H | WEST BROM | 17/3 | | 1 W 5-0 | 45,353 18 46 | Ditchburn Sanders | Ramsey Rickaby | Willis Millard | Nicholson Kennedy | Clarke Vernon | Burgess Barlow | Walters Allen | Bennett Dudley | Duquemin Richardson | Baily McCall | Medley Lee |

Duquemin 10, 55, 58, Bennett 61, [Baily 75]
Ref: R Burgess
Bennett and Duquemin are recalled in a bid to jump-start the stuttering Spurs attack and they have a field day. The 'Duke' grabs the headlines and a hat-trick, but Bennett terrorises the Albion too. For the finale, Murphy dribbles for 60 yards before teeing up Baily on the goal-line.

| 34 | A | FULHAM | 23/3 | | 1 W 1-0 | 47,391 16 48 | Ditchburn Black | Ramsey Bacuzzi | Willis Lowe R | Nicholson Quested | Clarke Taylor | Burgess Lowe E | Walters Stevens | Bennett Bowie | Duquemin Thomas | Baily Jezzard | Medley Campbell |

Murphy 47
Ref: W Edwards
It's been a very wet winter and Good Friday is just as waterlogged. The Lilywhites still manage delightful football on what appears to be an extension of the River Thames. The Cottagers rely more on heavy tackling, but still threaten a doggedly determined Spurs defence at the end.

| 35 | A | PORTSMOUTH | 24/3 | | 1 D 1-1 | 49,716 10 49 | Ditchburn Butler | Ramsey Stephen | Willis Ferrier | Nicholson Scoular | Clarke Froggatt | Burgess Dickinson | Walters Uphill | Bennett Harris | Duquemin Reid | Baily Phillips | Medley Galliard |

Uphill 44
Reid 6
Ref: E Vickery
A vicious wind adds an extra ingredient to the soggy conditions, but Portsmouth are unfazed as they race into a quick lead. Once more it is a recalled man who stars for Tottenham. Uphill replaces Bennett at inside-right and dispatches Burgess's free-kick to earn a merited 1-1 draw.

| 36 | H | FULHAM | 26/3 | | 1 W 2-1 | 51,862 16 51 | Ditchburn Black | Ramsey Bacuzzi | Withers Lowe R | Nicholson Quested | Clarke Taylor | Burgess Lowe E | Medley Stevens | Bennett Bowie | Duquemin Thomas | Baily Jezzard | Medley Campbell |

Bennett 39, Murphy 44
Jezzard 88
Ref: W Edwards
Withers replaces an unfit Willis, whilst Bennett bounces back from his brief rest. It is he who opens the scoring from a Ramsey free-kick, just before Medley tees up Murphy for number two. Spurs are four points clear of Man Utd, who have won ten out of their last eleven matches.

| 37 | H | EVERTON | 31/3 | | 1 W 3-0 | 46,651 19 53 | Ditchburn Sagar | Ramsey Moore | Willis Rankin | Nicholson Grant | Clarke Jones | Burgess Farrell | Walters Fielding | Bennett Potts | Duquemin Catterick | Baily Parker | Medley Eglington |

Walters 55, Murphy 63, Bennett 74
Ref: R Leafe
Lowly Everton defy their league position to match Spurs for the first half, but a neat passing move instigated by Nicholson leads to a home goal. The standard free-kick routine (Ramsey kicks to an onrushing Murphy) makes it 2-0, then Bennett deservedly poached the third goal.

| 38 | A | NEWCASTLE | 7/4 | | 1 W 1-0 | 41,241 6 55 | Ditchburn Fairbrother | Ramsey Cowell | Willis Corbett | Nicholson Stokoe | Clarke McNeil | Burgess Crowe | Walters Walker | Bennett Taylor | Duquemin Milburn | Baily Robledo G | Medley Mitchell |

Walters 7
Ref: H Evans
Spurs vary their usual free-kick routine. This time Willis takes it, but the result is still the same. The Newcastle defence stands like statues whilst Walters nips in to score. Spurs then defend stoutly to leave themselves six points clear of Man Utd with only four games remaining.

| 39 | H | HUDDERSFIELD | 14/4 | | 1 L 0-2 | 55,014 18 55 | Ditchburn Wheeler | Willis Gallogly | Withers Kelly | Nicholson McGarry | Clarke McEvoy | Burgess Boot | Walters McKenna | Bennett Glazzard | Duquemin Taylor | Baily Nightingale | Medley Metcalfe |

Glazzard 42, Nightingale 48
Ref: G Tedds
Both teams are missing players on international duty (Ramsey and Hassall). The Terriers make it a hat-trick of wins over Spurs by matching them in every department and then outscoring them. Man Utd narrow the gap to four points, with Blackpool a further two points behind them.

| 40 | A | MIDDLESBROUGH | 21/4 | | 1 D 1-1 | 36,689 4 56 | Ditchburn Ugolini | Willis Robinson | Withers Dicks | Nicholson Bell | Clarke Blenkinsopp | Burgess Brown | Walters Delapenha | Bennett Fitzsimmons | Murphy Mannion | Baily Spuhler | Medley Walker |

Murphy 22
Spuhler 30
Ref: F Thurman
A Middlesbrough side without Mannion should be an easier proposition, but the Lilywhites have the championship jitters. They are roasted in the first half, but take the lead through a fortuitous lob from Murphy. Boro deservedly level and then dominate the attack in the second half.

| 41 | H | SHEFFIELD WED | 28/4 | | 1 W 1-0 | 46,645 22 58 | Ditchburn McIntosh | Ramsey Jackson | Willis Curtis | Nicholson Henry | Clarke Packard | Burgess Witcomb | Walters Finney | Murphy Sewell | Duquemin Woodhead | Baily Froggatt | Medley Rickett |

Duquemin 45
Ref: G Iliffe
Wednesday have spent £34,500 on Jackie Sewell to try to beat the drop, but they are unable to prevent Spurs collecting their first-ever championship. A typically slick interchange between Burgess, Baily and Medley results in the 'Duke' crowning Tottenham with the winner.

| 42 | H | LIVERPOOL | 5/5 | | 1 W 3-1 | 49,072 9 60 | Ditchburn Ashcroft | Ramsey Lambert | Willis Spicer | Nicholson Jones | Clarke Hughes | Burgess Paisley | Walters Payne | Murphy Taylor | Duquemin Stubbins | Baily Done | Medley Brierley |

Walters 56, Murphy 64, 72
Stubbins 85
Ref: S Law
Spurs receive the championship trophy from Mr Drewry – President of the Football League after the game but, before that, the two teams end the season with a crackerjack match. In one enchanting 15-minute spell, the ball is continuously in play without any stoppages whatsoever.

Home 55,509
Away 43,289
Average 55,509

LEAGUE DIVISION 1 (CUP-TIES)   Manager: Arthur Rowe   SEASON 1950-51

FA Cup

			F-A	H-T	Scorers, Times, and Referees	1	2	3	4	5	6	7	8	9	10	11
3	A	HUDDERSFIELD	1 L	0-2	0-0	Ditchburn	Ramsey	Willis	Nicholson	Clarke	Burgess	Walters	Bennett	Duquemin	Baily	Medley
6/1		25,390 20			Taylor 75, Glazzard 79	*Wheeler*	*Gallogly*	*Kelly*	*Battye*	*McEvoy*	*Boot*	*Glazzard*	*Hassall*	*Taylor*	*Nightingale*	*Metcalfe*
					Ref: R Griffiths											

Dense fog and a waterlogged pitch threaten to give 7,000 Spurs fans a wasted journey as the game is in doubt till 45 minutes before kick-off. Town's robustness sinks Tottenham's daintier passing game that literally gets bogged down. A coach crash on the way home kills two fans.

Festival of Britain

			F-A	H-T	Scorers	1	2	3	4	5	6	7	8	9	10	11
	H	FC AUSTRIA	L 0-1	0-1	*Ocvirk 11*	Ditchburn	Withers	Willis	Nicholson	Clarke	Burgess	Walters	Murphy	Duquemin	Baily	Medley
7/5		30,000														

FC Austria mesmerise Spurs with an advanced demonstration of 'push and run'. No pass seems to exceed ten yards and the Austrians seem totally unhurried in everything they do. The goal comes from a threaded pass through Spurs' defence, met by a twisting half-volley on the run.

			F-A	H-T	Scorers	1	2	3	4	5	6	7	8	9	10	11
	H	BOR DORTMUND	W 2-1	2-0	Murphy 11, Baily 27	Ditchburn	Ramsey	Willis	Brittan	Clarke	Marchi	Walters	Bennett	McLennan	Baily	Murphy
12/5		29,000			*Michalek 67*											

The East Germans aren't as exquisite as the Austrians, but play a similar style of football. They are beaten by Murphy's speed, then Baily's 20-yard netbuster. Ditchburn is substituted on 42 minutes with a fractured finger. The 5ft 6½ full-back Withers does remarkably well in his place.

152

League Table

		P	W	D	L	F(H)	A(H)	W	D	L	F(A)	A(A)	Pts
1	TOTTENHAM	42	17	2	2	54	21	8	8	5	28	23	60
2	Manchester U	42	14	4	3	42	16	10	4	7	32	24	56
3	Blackpool	42	12	6	3	43	19	8	4	9	36	34	50
4	Newcastle	42	10	6	5	36	22	8	7	6	26	31	49
5	Arsenal	42	11	5	5	47	28	8	4	9	26	28	47
6	Middlesbro	42	12	7	2	51	25	6	4	11	25	40	47
7	Portsmouth	42	8	10	3	39	30	8	5	8	32	38	47
8	Bolton	42	11	2	8	31	20	8	5	8	33	41	45
9	Liverpool	42	11	5	5	28	25	5	6	10	25	34	43
10	Burnley	42	9	7	5	27	16	5	7	9	21	27	42
11	Derby	42	10	5	6	53	33	6	3	12	28	42	40
12	Sunderland	42	8	9	4	30	21	4	7	10	33	52	40
13	Stoke	42	10	5	6	28	19	3	9	9	22	40	40
14	Wolves	42	9	3	9	44	30	6	5	10	30	31	38
15	Aston Villa	42	9	6	6	39	29	3	7	11	27	39	37
16	West Brom	42	7	4	10	30	27	6	7	8	23	34	37
17	Charlton	42	9	4	8	35	31	5	5	11	28	49	37
18	Fulham	42	8	5	8	35	37	5	6	10	17	31	37
19	Huddersfield	42	8	4	9	40	40	7	2	12	24	52	36
20	Chelsea	42	9	4	8	31	25	3	4	14	22	40	32
21	Sheffield Wed	42	9	6	6	43	32	3	2	16	21	51	32
22	Everton	42	7	5	9	26	35	5	3	13	22	51	32
		924	218	114	130	832	581	130	114	218	581	832	924

Appearances and Goals

Player	Lge	FAC	Lge Goals	Tot
Baily, Eddie	40	1	12	12
Bennett, Les	25	1	7	7
Brittan, Colin	8			
Burgess, Ron	35	1	2	2
Clarke, Harry	42	1		
Ditchburn, Ted	42	1		
Duquemin, Len	33		14	14
McClellan, Sid	7		3	3
Medley, Les	35	1	11	11
Murphy, Peter	25		9	9
Nicholson, Bill	41	1	1	1
Ramsey, Alf	40	1	4	4
Scarth, Jimmy	1			
Tickridge, Sid	1			
Uphill, Dennis	2		1	1
Walters, Sonny	40	1	15	15
Willis, Arthur	39	1		
Withers, Charlie	4			
Wright, Alex	2		1	1
(own-goals)			2	2
19 players used	462		82	82

Odds & ends

Double wins: (7) Aston Villa, Bolton, Chelsea, Everton, Fulham, Newcastle, West Brom.
Double losses: (1) Huddersfield.
Won from behind: (3) Bolton (a), Bolton (h), Aston Villa (a).
Lost from in front: (1) Manchester U (a).
High spots: Proving the worth of Rowe's 'Push and Run' by winning the Championship.
The stylish, attractive way the title was won.
The fans that made Spurs the best-supported team in the land.
'Push and Run'; bringing football into the modern era at last.
Low spots: Falling at the first fence in the FA Cup.
Losing to Huddersfield three times in three games.
The death of two fans in a coach crash.

Hat-tricks: (3) Baily, Duquemin, Medley.
Ever-presents: (2) Clarke, Ditchburn.
Leading scorer: Walters (15)

LEAGUE DIVISION 1   Manager: Bill Nicholson   SEASON 1960-61

No	Date			Att	Pos	Pt	F-A	H-T	1	2	3	4	5	6	7	8	9	10	11
1	H 20/8	EVERTON	53,395		1 22	W 2	2-0	0-0	Brown Dunlop	Baker Parker	Henry Jones	Blanchflower Gabriel	Norman Labone	Mackay Meagan	Jones Lill	White Collins	Smith R Harris	Allen Vernon	Dyson Ring
		Scorers, Times, and Referees: Allen 86, Smith 87 Ref: E Crawford																		
		The match seems destined to end 0-0 when the ref astutely plays advantage when Smith is hacked down in the box. Allen tucks away the loose ball, then Smith soon makes it 2-0 with a diving header. Of the dramatic finish, Blanchflower says 'Well, it makes it more exciting that way.'																		
2	A 22/8	BLACKPOOL	27,656		1 16	W 4	3-1	2-0	Brown Waiters	Baker Armfield	Henry Martin	Blanchflower Kelly J	Norman Gratrix	Mackay Durie	Medwin Matthews	White Mudie	Smith R Charnley	Allen Kaye	Dyson Campbell
		Scorers: Dyson 9, 55, Medwin 34 Mudie 56 Ref: N Hough																		
		Ex-jockey Dyson launches his 5ft 2in frame above the Blackpool defence to head the first goal. Kaye misses a penalty for the home side after Baker fouled Charnley on 31 minutes. Medwin ensures the points with a fierce drive, then Dyson wraps things up with a close-range shot.																		
3	A 27/8	BLACKBURN	26,700		1 7	W 6	4-1	3-0	Brown Jones	Baker England	Henry Eckersley	Blanchflower Clayton	Norman Woods	Mackay McGrath	Medwin Douglas	White Dobing	Smith R Dougan	Allen Crowe	Dyson McLeod
		Scorers: Smith 6, 15, Allen 18, Dyson 47 Dougan 89 Ref: J Carr																		
		Spurs slam the ball three times past Rovers' goalie Jones before his team have woken up. To their great credit they come to life to match the visitors for the rest of the game, but the result is never in doubt. Tottenham's neat, almost casual passing is the undoing of workaday Rovers.																		
4	H 31/8	BLACKPOOL	46,684		1 15	W 8	3-1	1-1	Brown Waiters	Baker Armfield	Henry Martin	Blanchflower Kelly J	Norman Gratrix	Mackay Durie	Medwin Hill	White Lea	Smith R Charnley	Allen Mudie	Dyson Kaye
		Scorers: Smith 4, 75, 82 Lea 35 Ref: R Mann																		
		Smith sticks his head in the path of a Blanchflower shot to score his 131st league and cup goal, to break George Hunt's pre-war record. The Seasiders have replaced the aged guile of Matthews with the youthful speed of Hill and give Spurs a real test. Smith's hat-trick kills the game.																		
5	H 3/9	MANCHESTER U	55,445		1 20	W 10	4-1	2-1	Brown Gregg	Baker Foulkes	Henry Brennan	Blanchflower Setters	Norman Haydock	Mackay Nicholson	Medwin Quixall	White Giles	Smith R Dawson	Allen Viollett	Dyson Charlton
		Scorers: Smith 7, 85, Allen 20, 65 Viollett 43 Ref: A Moore																		
		A sloppy pass in defence by Setters gifts Spurs an early goal. Teams have to be at their best to match Spurs, who play with a machine-like efficiency. United do this and the scoreline flatters Hotspur, though a robust tackle that flattens and winds Mackay helps the Red Devils' cause.																		
6	A 7/9	BOLTON	41,151		1 17	W 12	2-1	0-1	Brown Hopkinson	Baker Hartle	Henry Banks	Blanchflower Stanley	Norman Higgins	Mackay Edwards	Medwin Birch	White Hill	Smith R McAdams	Allen Parry	Dyson Holden
		Scorers: Allen 63, White 73 McAdams 3 Ref: R Langdale																		
		A deflected shot by McAdams gives the Trotters a shock lead and Tottenham's 100% record is in some doubt until Bolton's left-back Banks is injured on 55 minutes. Allen immediately equalises and White nets the winner. Saul (aged 17) is only denied a debut goal by the woodwork.																		
7	A 10/9	ARSENAL	60,088		1 8	W 14	3-2	2-0	Brown Kelsey	Baker Wills	Henry McCullough	Blanchflower Ward	Norman Sneddon	Mackay Docherty	Medwin Clapton	White Bloomfield	Saul Herd	Allen Kane	Dyson Henderson
		Scorers: Saul 12, Dyson 22, Allen 73 Herd 62, Ward 67 Ref: J Williams																		
		Saul beats two and fires home in true 'Boys Own' fashion, and then Dyson makes it 2-0 to kill the game. Though a poor side, Arsenal use the frenetic pace and reduced skill of the derby game to stun Spurs with two killer goals. Allen steals the winner, though he may have been offside.																		
8	H 14/9	BOLTON	43,559		1 19	W 16	3-1	1-1	Brown Hopkinson	Baker Hartle	Henry Farrimond	Blanchflower Hennin	Norman Edwards	Mackay Stanley	Medwin Birch	White Hill	Smith R McAdams	Allen Parry	Dyson Holden
		Scorers: Smith 24, 85, Blanchflower 65p McAdams 7 Ref: F. Clarke																		
		The ref awards Spurs the penalty that puts them in front. But even the Spurs players don't know why. Apparently, Dyson was fouled. Later, Bolton's goalie Hopkinson refuses to take a goal-kick unless a policeman is stationed behind his goal. He alleges litter is being thrown at him.																		
9	A 17/9	LEICESTER	30,129		1 16	W 18	2-1	1-1	Brown Banks	Baker King	Henry Norman	Blanchflower McLintock	Norman Knapp	Mackay Appleton	Medwin Riley	White Walsh	Smith R Leek	Allen Cheesbrough	Dyson Wills
		Scorers: Smith 18, 54 Riley 29 Ref J Mitchell																		
		Tottenham's team almost seems to operate on automatic pilot, such is the level of understanding between them, but they don't seem hungry for goals. Though they equal Hull's 1948 record of nine wins from the season's start, the record nearly ends when City come close at the death.																		
10	H 24/9	ASTON VILLA	61,356		1 9	W 20	6-2	4-0	Brown Sims	Baker Neal	Henry Winton	Blanchflower Crowe	Norman Morrall	Mackay Deakin	Jones MacEwan	White Thomson	Smith R Hitchens	Dyson Wylie	Burrows
		Scorers: White 7,19, Smith 27, Dys 30, Al'n 55, MacEw'n 65, Hitchens 80 (Mackay 85) Ref: L Hamer																		
		Villa haven't beaten Spurs in any of the 18 meetings since the war and that record continues as a thrashing is ensured after just 30 minutes. Even after Tottenham have eased up and the Villains make a token comeback, Hotspur lift the tempo to allow Mackay to steer in number six.																		

154

#	H/A	Date	Opponent	Res	Score	Att	Pos	Pts	Scorers / Lineup details
11	A	1/10	WOLVERHAMPTON	W	4-0	53,036	6	22	Jones 35, Blanchflower 45, Allen 46, Brown [Dyson 60] — Ref: H Callaghan
12	H	12/10	MANCHESTER C	D	1-1	58,916	8	23	Smith 27 / Colbridge 50 — Ref: G Pullin
13	A	15/10	NOTT'M FOREST	W	4-0	37,198	21	25	White 7, Mackay 19, Jones 25, 57 — Ref: J Bullough
14	A	29/10	NEWCASTLE	W	4-3	51,369	17	27	Norman 34, White 51, Jones 58, White 32, 36, Hughes 62 [Smith 86] — Ref: F Stringer
15	H	2/11	CARDIFF	W	3-2	47,605	18	29	Dyson 35, Medwin 41, Blanch'r 51pl / Donnelly 19, 86 — Ref: K Tuck
16	H	5/11	FULHAM	W	5-1	56,270	8	31	Allen 22, 83, Jones 28, 75, White 80 / Leggat 52 — Ref: L Callaghan
17	A	12/11	SHEFFIELD WED	L	1-2	56,363	2	31	Norman 42 / Griffin 40, Fantham 69 — Ref: R Leafe
18	H	19/11	BIRMINGHAM	W	6-0	46,010	14	33	White 3, Dyson 9, 76, Jones 15, 86, [Smith 82pl] — Ref: G Thorpe
19	A	26/11	WEST BROM	W	3-1	37,800	19	35	Smith 22, 28, Allen 35 / Howe 36 — Ref: J McLoughlin
20	H	3/12	BURNLEY	D	4-4	58,737	6	36	Norman 18, Jones 19, 21, Mackay 32 / Connelly 43, 72, Robson 56, Pointer 61 Blacklaw — Ref: R Windle
21	A	10/12	PRESTON	W	1-0	21,657	21	38	White 16 — Ref: H Hackney

Lineups (Tottenham / Opposition)

11 Wolverhampton (A): Brown; Baker, Henry; Blanchflower, Norman, Marchi; Jones, White, Smith R, Allen, Dyson / Sidebottom; Showell, Harris; Clamp, Stuart, Flowers; Deeley, Broadbent, Farmer, Mason, Horne.
Wolves may have been the best team of the last few years, but their long-ball style attack and offside trap defence seems crude compared to the more sophisticated continental style of Spurs. Marchi takes Mackay's place (food poisoning) and Blanchflower's 25-yarder is the best goal.

12 Manchester C (H): Brown; Baker, Henry; Blanchflower, Norman, Marchi; Jones, White, Smith R, Allen, Dyson / Trautmann; Betts, Barnes; Barlow, Plenderleith, Shawcross; Colbridge, Law, Hannah, Hayes, Colbridge.
The Man City team coach is held up in heavy traffic and arrives only ten minutes before kick-off. When White guides a precision cross onto Smith's head, it seems all over, but the 100% record ends when Colbridge accurately rifles home a crossed ball. For once, Spurs seem to panic.

13 Nott'm Forest (A): Brown; Baker, Henry; Blanchflower, Norman, Mackay; Jones, White, Smith R, Allen, Dyson / Thomson; Patrick, McDonald; Whitefoot, McKinlay, Iley; Rowland, Bowden, Julians, Gray, Le Flem.
Despite ex-Spurs star Jim Iley trying to catch his former club off guard with some early long-range shooting, the visitors aren't going to repeat the mistakes of the last game. White's clever chip opens the scoring and it's child's play to take two points off the outclassed Forest players.

14 Newcastle (A): Brown; Baker, Henry; Blanchflower, Norman, Mackay; Jones, White, Smith R, Allen, Dyson / Harvey; Keith, McMichael; Scoular, Stokoe, Bell; Hughes, Woods, White, Allchurch, Mitchell.
A breathtaking ding-dong game in which the lead switches rapidly. There is no surprise that Spurs take home the points, but Newcastle feel aggrieved the linesman was flagging for offside when Jones got his goal. Smith breaks Geordie hearts by snatching the late winner.

15 Cardiff (H): Brown; Baker, Henry; Blanchflower, Norman, Mackay; Jones, White, Smith R, Allen, Dyson / Vearncombe; Harrington, Edwards; Gammon, Malloy, Baker; Medwin, Walsh, Sullivan, Tapscott, Hogg.
It's Cardiff who play the more attractive football and they wouldn't have been flattered with a win. Spurs seem to be merely going through the motions and don't look safe even when an accidental handball gives them a penalty to make it 3-1.

16 Fulham (H): Brown; Baker, Henry; Blanchflower, Norman, Mackay; Jones, White, Smith R, Allen, Dyson / Macedo; Cohen, Langley; Mullery, Bentley, Edwards; Key, Hill, Cook, Haynes, Leggat.
If anyone could have aided the industrious Johnny Haynes up front, then Fulham might have made it an exciting finish. As it is, Tottenham demonstrate clinical efficiency in tucking away their chances in the first half, before hitting top form to make it a thrashing in the second.

17 Sheffield Wed (A): Brown; Baker, Henry; Blanchflower, Norman, Mackay; Jones, White, Smith R, Allen, Dyson / McLaren; Johnson, Megson; McAnearney, Swan, Kay; Griffin, Craig, Ellis, Fantham, Finney.
Griffin's opening goal doesn't seem to matter much when Norman lashes home a quick equaliser. Fantham restores the lead to the Owls and then Spurs lose their discipline and indulge in rough-house tactics. Poor McLaren in goal is knocked out by a charging Dyson near the end.

18 Birmingham (H): Brown; Baker, Henry; Blanchflower, Norman, Mackay; Jones, White, Smith R, Allen, Dyson / Withers; Sissons, Allen; Watts, Smith, Neal; Hellawell, Gordon, Singer, Bloomfield, Taylor.
Spurs race into a three-goal lead, then seem to play with City like a cat does with a half-dead mouse, knowing they're too weak to respond. Then when Bloomfield (their new signing from Arsenal) has burned himself out in attack, they finish the job off with another three-goal blitz.

19 West Brom (A): Brown; Baker, Henry; Blanchflower, Norman, Mackay; Jones, White, Smith R, Allen, Dyson / Wallace; Cram, Williams S; Drury, Kennedy, Robson; Williams G, Jackson, Howe, Kevan, Williams G.
Playing England full-back Don Howe as a striker, Albion match Spurs until Smith opens the scoring in an offside position, though White's clever back-heel to him may have brushed a defender's legs. The win means Tottenham are now nine points clear at the top of the division.

20 Burnley (H): Brown; Baker, Henry; Blanchflower, Norman, Mackay; Jones, White, Smith R, Allen, Dyson / Blacklaw; Angus, Elder; Joyce, Cummings, Miller; Connelly, McIlroy, Pointer, Robson, Pilkington.
A swirling wind, driving rain and a muddy pitch don't affect Spurs as they shake off early Burnley pressure and score three in three minutes. At 4-0 it seems all over, then Burnley seem to realise it's their title that's slipping away and they stage one of the all-time great comebacks.

21 Preston (A): Brown; Baker, Henry; Blanchflower, Norman, Mackay; Jones, White, Smith R, Allen, Dyson / Else; Cunningham, O'Neill; Fullam, Singleton, Wylie; Mayers, Thompson T, Alston, Saul, Thompson P.
Relegation-haunted Preston actually try to outplay Tottenham with style and panache. Unfortunately they haven't the guile to break through a resolute defence. Spurs score when Norman nods a corner into White's path. There's no goal shortage for the reserves. They beat Ipswich 9-1.

LEAGUE DIVISION 1 Manager: Bill Nicholson SEASON 1960-61

No	Date		Att	Pos	Pt	F-A	H-T	Scorers, Times, and Referees	1	2	3	4	5	6	7	8	9	10	11
22	A	EVERTON		1	W	3-1	2-0	White 36, Allen 39, Mackay 60	Brown	Baker	Henry	Blanchflower	Norman	Mackay	Jones	White	Smith R	Allen	Dyson
	17/12		61,052	2	40			Wignall 47	Dunlop	Parker	Thomson	Gabriel	Labone	Harris	Bingham	Wignall	Young	Collins	Temple
								Ref: A Holland											
								Thick fog slowly envelops Goodison Park during the game, but by then the home fans have seen quite enough of the champions-elect. The moves which lead to both first-half goals are started by Blanchflower, whilst Everton's retort is squashed by a 35-yard Mackay blockbuster.											
23	H	WEST HAM		1	W	2-0	1-0	White 25, Dyson 84	Brown	Baker	Henry	Blanchflower	Norman	Mackay	Jones	White	Smith R	Allen	Dyson
	24/12		54,930	7	42				Rhodes	Bond	Lyall	Malcolm	Brown	Moore	Grice	Woosnam	Dunmore	Dick	Musgrove
								Ref: R Leafe											
								Either the players have had too much early Christmas pud or they're wearing lead-lined boots on the muddy pitch, but much of this game is played at a walking pace. An injury to Jones blunts the Spurs attack in the second half. Smith tees up both goals by literally using his head.											
24	A	WEST HAM		1	W	3-0	2-0	Brown 24 (og), Allen 44, White 81	Hollowbread	Baker	Henry	Blanchflower	Norman	Mackay	Medwin	White	Smith R	Allen	Dyson
	26/12		34,481	8	44					Bond	Lyall	Malcolm	Brown	Moore	Grice	Woosnam	Dunmore	Dick	Musgrove
								Ref: R Mann											
								With Hollowbread and Medwin replacing the injured Brown and Jones, Spurs look much livelier at a packed Upton Park. The first goal is credited to Brown when Allen's shot bobbles in off him. Allen's neat control and shot makes it 2-0, and White slips through at the end for 3-0.											
25	H	BLACKBURN		1	W	5-2	1-1	Smith 39, 66, Allen 57, 62 Blanch' 59	Brown	Baker	Henry	Blanchflower	Norman	Marchi	Medwin	White	Smith R	Allen	Dyson
	31/12		48,742	11	46			Douglas 16, Dobing 79	Reeves	Taylor	Bray	McEvoy	Woods	Clayton	Douglas	Dobing	Dougan	Crowe	Macleod
								Ref: R Jordan											
								Blackburn have plenty of possession before the break, but little penetration, apart from Douglas's opportunistic drive. Any thoughts of an upset are blasted away in a devastating nine-minute spell when Spurs grab four goals. It's the Cup next week and talk of the double has now started.											
26	A	MANCHESTER U		1	L	0-2	0-1	Stiles 14, Pearson 73	Brown	Barton	Henry	Blanchflower	Norman	Mackay	Smith J	White	Smith R	Allen	Dyson
	16/1		65,295	8	46				Gregg	Brennan	Cantwell	Setters	Foulkes	Nicholson	Quixall	Stiles	Dawson	Pearson	Charlton
								Ref: W Surtees											
								Barton and John Smith replace injured players. These changes cannot excuse the defeat as United play the second half with Dawson in goal and goalkeeper Gregg, nursing an injured shoulder, goes up front. Unbelievably, Gregg creates the second with a classy back-heel to Pearson.											
27	H	ARSENAL		1	W	4-2	3-1	Allen 10, 60, Blanchflower 23p,	Brown	Baker	Henry	Blanchflower	Norman	Mackay	Jones	White	Smith R	Allen	Dyson
	21/1		65,251	7	48			Henderson 8, Haverty 64 (Smith 43)	McClelland	Magill	McCullough	Neill	Young	Docherty	Clapton	Eastham	Herd	Henderson	Haverty
								Ref: A Ellis											
								It may be regarded as the worst-ever Arsenal team, but they still punish Spurs when they leave too much space. The massive home support is soon relieved as normal service is resumed. The Gunners soon tire and captain Tommy Docherty is booked for arguing. Surely some mistake?											
28	H	LEICESTER		1	L	2-3	1-2	Allen 42, Blanchflower 47p	Brown	Baker	Henry	Blanchflower	Norman	Mackay	Jones	White	Smith R	Allen	Dyson
	4/2		53,627	7	48			Leek 31, Walsh 44, 65	Banks	Chalmers	Norman	McLintock	King	Appleton	Riley	Walsh	Leek	Keyworth	Wills
								Ref: K Dagnall											
								The Foxes break into the White Hart Lane Co-op and savage the Cockerel. A combination of tough tackling, long passing and no little skill is enough against a jaded Spurs' team to end the unbeaten home record. The penalty is given when Smith is pushed into the penalty-area mud.											
29	A	ASTON VILLA		1	W	2-1	0-0	Smith 46, Dyson 56	Brown	Baker	Henry	Blanchflower	Norman	Mackay	Jones	White	Smith R	Allen	Dyson
	18/2		50,810	7	50			Lynn 71p	Sims	Lynn	Neal	Crowe	Dugdale	Deakin	MacEwan	O'Neill	Hitchens	Thomson	McParland
								Ref: K Collinge											
								In a rehearsal for next week's Cup-tie, Smith opens the scoring 30 seconds into the second half when he heads home Allen's cross. Dyson volleys in White's centre for 2-0, but then there's controversy after Villa get a penalty for obstruction. Spurs say it's their man who was fouled.											
30	H	WOLVERHAMPTON		1	D	1-1	1-1	Smith 10	Brown	Baker	Henry	Blanchflower	Norman	Mackay	Jones	White	Smith R	Allen	Dyson
	22/2		62,261	2	51			Farmer 23	Finlayson	Stuart	Showell	Clamp	Slater	Flowers	Deeley	Murray	Farmer	Broadbent	Durand
								Ref: J Williams											
								In what almost appears to be a premature championship-decider, Spurs get too cocky after taking an early lead. The defenders casually allow themselves to get caught in possession and that gives Farmer the opportunity to make hay whilst Wolves' title ambitions remain shining.											
31	A	MANCHESTER C		1	W	1-0	1-0	Medwin 60	Brown	Baker	Henry	Blanchflower	Marchi	Mackay	Medwin	White	Smith R	Allen	Dyson
	25/2		40,278	17	53				Fleet	Leivers	Betts	Shawcross	Plenderleith	Oakes	Colbridge	Law	Barlow	Hayes	Wagstaffe
								Ref: P Rhodes											
								Norman (groin strain) and Jones (septic throat) force a rare change to Tottenham's line-up. On a mudbath of a pitch, the Citizens match Spurs until outside-left Hayes becomes a limping passenger after 40 minutes. Medwin's header means they are now nine points clear at the summit.											

156

#	H/A	Date	Opponent	W/L/D	Score	Pos	Pts	Attend	Scorers & Notes
32	A	11/3	CARDIFF	L	2-3	6	53	58,000	Dyson 3, Allen 21; Hogg 10, Walsh 51, Tapscott 52. Ref: E Jennings
33	H	22/3	NEWCASTLE	L	1-2	19	53	46,470	Allen 40; Allchurch 65, Scanlon 79. Ref: K Stokes
34	A	25/3	FULHAM	D	0-0	17	54	38,536	Ref: H Horner
35	H	31/3	CHELSEA	W	4-2	14	56	65,032	Jones 49, 55, Allen 65, Saul 82; Brabrook 87, Tindall 89. Ref: G Pullin
36	H	1/4	PRESTON	W	5-0	22	58	46,325	White 4, Jones 11, 45, 52, Saul 15. Ref: M Fussey
37	A	3/4	CHELSEA	W	3-2	15	60	57,103	Smith 7, Medwin 67, Norman 75; Blunstone 47, Greaves 55. Ref: J Kelly
38	A	8/4	BIRMINGHAM	W	3-2	14	62	40,960	Smith 2, Allen 25, White 32; Harris 37p, 48. Ref: L Tirebuck
39	H	17/4	SHEFFIELD WED	W	2-1	2	64	61,200	Smith 42, Allen 45; Megson 28. Ref: T Dawes
40	A	22/4	BURNLEY	L	2-4	5	64	28,397	Baker 19, Smith 39; Harris 60, 84, McIlroy 70, Robson 88 Blacklaw. Ref: A Holland
41	H	26/4	NOTT'M FOREST	W	1-0		66	35,743	Medwin 64. Ref: P Carr
42	H	29/4	WEST BROM	L	1-2		66	52,054	Smith 49; Kevan 4, Robson 74. Ref: J Williams

Home 53,315 / Away 43,717 Average

32 CARDIFF — Brown / Baker Nicolls / Henry Harrington / Blanchflower Hole / Norman Malloy / Mackay Baker / Jones Walsh / White Moore / Smith R Tapscott / Allen Donnelly / Dyson Hogg
Any side that can come back from twice being behind for the remainder of the match, thoroughly deserve the two points. The semi-final looms for Spurs. Dyson shut out the most lethal attack in football for the rest of the match, can then take the lead by scoring twice in a minute; then can

33 NEWCASTLE — Brown / Baker Keith / Henry McMichael / Blanchflower Neale / Norman McGrath / Mackay Bell / Jones Hodgson / White Allchurch / Smith R White / Allen Harrower / Dyson Scanlon
Relegation-haunted Newcastle are overrun in the first half and are lucky only to be a goal down at the break, especially when Blanchflower sees his penalty saved by the outstanding Hollins (making his debut in the Newcastle goal). Brown misses Scanlon's cross for their winner.

34 FULHAM — Brown / Baker Cohen / Henry Langley / Blanchflower Mullery / Norman Dodgin / Mackay Lowe / Jones Leggatt / White O'Connell / Smith R Cook / Allen Haynes / Dyson Johnson
Mackay and Smith are missing, but Marchi and Saul are more than adequate replacements. It just seems a general jadedness that permeates through Tottenham's ranks. They have lots of possession, but no rapier thrusts near to goal. Sheff Wed are only three points behind them now.

35 CHELSEA — Brown / Baker Sillett J / Henry Sillett P / Blanchflower Venables / Norman Scott / Marchi Anderton / Jones Brabrook / White Greaves / Smith R Tindall / Allen Tambling / Dyson Harrison
For 54 minutes it's a (lack of) action replay of the Fulham game. Then the nervousness is ended with a couple of quick, firm drives from Jones. Allen dances through Chelsea's back line for the third and young Saul makes it four. Norman and Henry collide twice to let Chelsea in.

36 PRESTON — Brown / Baker Cunningham / Henry O'Neill / Blanchflower Wylie / Norman Singleton / Mackay O'Farrell / Jones Dagger / White Fullam / Smith R Alston / Allen Sneddon / Dyson Thompson
When Preston's reserve keeper Kelly fumbles a soft shot from White into his own net, the visitors visibly surrender. The only disappointment for the Spurs fans is that they don't go on to get double figures. Jones' first goal of his hat-trick is Tottenham 100th league goal of the season.

37 CHELSEA — Brown / Baker Sillett J / Henry Harris / Blanchflower Venables / Norman Scott / Mackay Anderton / Jones Blunstone / White Greaves / Smith R Brabrook / Allen Tambling / Dyson Harrison
Despite conceding an early goal, then losing Brabrook (dislocated shoulder) before half-time, Chelsea fight back and take the lead through Jimmy Greaves (who was booked when an earlier 'goal' was ruled offside). Norman's header lifts Spurs five points clear of Sheffield Wed.

38 BIRMINGHAM — Brown / Baker Farmer / Henry Allen / Blanchflower Hennessey / Norman Smith / Mackay Neal / Jones Hellawell / White Orritt / Smith R Harris / Allen Bloomfield / Dyson Taylor
For the third game running Spurs take an early lead. Two more first-half goals seem to have killed the game, but when Bloomfield is hacked down in the box it sparks a Blues revival. The Whites hold firm to quash the comeback at 3-2, then they maintain possession until the finish.

39 SHEFFIELD WED — Brown / Baker Johnson / Henry Megson / Blanchflower Hill / Norman Swan / Mackay Kay / Jones Finney / White Craig / Smith R Ellis / Allen Fantham / Dyson Wilkinson
Wednesday have to win to stop Spurs clinching the title. The title-winner comes when Norman nods a ball to Allen who volleys home. Johnson and Mackay are both booked rounded Megson to score.

40 BURNLEY — Brown / Baker Angus / Henry Elder / Blanchflower Joyce / Norman Cummings / Mackay Miller / Jones Connelly / Medwin McIlroy / Smith R Pointer / Allen Robson / Dyson Harris
With the League championship in the bag, the Cup beckoning, and two goals to the good, nobody can blame Spurs for easing off the gas. Just like the last league meeting, however, Burnley sting Spurs with a four-goal comeback to avenge (slightly) the pain of the FA Cup defeat.

41 NOTT'M FOREST — Brown / Baker Patrick / Henry Palmer / Blanchflower Whitefoot / Norman McKinlay / Marchi Iley / Medwin Rowland / White Booth / Smith R Vowden / Allen Quigley / Dyson Le Flem
Tottenham treat Forest's goal like a shooting range in the second half and Medwin eventually hits the target to equal Arsenal's record points haul of 66 (Spurs already hold the Div 2 record of 70). Forest ruled the first half though, and Vowden should have levelled the game late on.

42 WEST BROM — Brown / Baker Howe / Henry Williams / Blanchflower Robson / Norman Jones / Mackay Drury / Jones Jackson / White Hope / Smith R Lovatt / Allen Kevan / Dyson Clark
A draw would break Arsenal's 30-year record of 66 points in a season, but again the pre-Cup final jitters strike. In the end it's Spurs who are lucky to avoid a mauling as the Throstles strike the woodwork three times. The winner is a 30-yard screamer that Brown doesn't even see.

LEAGUE DIVISION 1 (CUP-TIES)   Manager: Bill Nicholson   SEASON 1960-61

Friendlies

			F-A	H-T	Scorers, Times, and Referees	1	2	3	4	5	6	7	8	9	10	11
H	ARMY XI		L 3-5	0-1	Allen 55, Yeats 73 (og), Aitchison 84	Brown	Baker	Henry	Dodge	Norman	Marchi	Aitchison	Collins	Saul	Allen	Dyson
24/10		5,947			Cro' 8p, 66, Byr' 48, Syd' 59, Smith 69 Ogston		Hill	Ferguson	Scott	Yeats	Smith J	Strong	Crowe	Byrne	Peacock	Sydenham
					Ref: W Eccles											

The Army's team contains four England Under-23 players, a Scottish Under-23 (future Liverpool legend Ron Yeats), and Pte P J Smith (RAMC) of Tottenham. They dismantle a Spurs defence of Brown, Baker, Henry and Norman in a way that no First Division outfit has yet managed.

H	DINAMO TBILISI		W 5-2	2-1	Medwin 18, 54 Mackay 42, 50	Brown	Baker	Henry	Blanchflower	Norman	Mackay	Medwin	White	Smith R	Allen	Dyson
14/11		38,649			Barkaya 32, 87 [Dyson 63]	Katrikadze	Sichinava	Chokheli	Voronin	Toraidze	Yamanidze	Melashvili	Barkaya	Kaloyrov	Gogoberidze	Meshki
					Ref: R Leafe											

The Army's team contains four England Under-23 players, a Scottish Under-23 (future Liverpool legend Ron Yeats), and Pte P J Smith (RAMC) of Tottenham. They dismantle a Spurs defence of Brown, Baker, Henry and Norman in a way that no First Division outfit has yet managed.

Spurs seem to be devoid of ideas on how to win this match and rely on man-to-man marking and an efficient offside trap to try to keep the score respectable. The exception is Meshki who proves the Russians are natural left-wingers. Mackay scores twice and creates Medwin's goal.

| A | FEYENOORD | | W 2-1 | 2-0 | Allen 16, Medwin 35 | Brown | Baker | Henry | Blanchflower | Norman | Mackay | Medwin | White | Smith R | Allen | Dyson |
| 15/5 | | 40,000 | | | Unknown 89 | | | | | | | | | | | |

Spurs get a taster of next season's European Cup when they take on Dutch champions Feyenoord in a tour match. An entertaining game ends with Spurs deservedly edging out Feyenoord with panache and sharp finishing. Smith (England) and Jones (Wales) are on international duty.

FA Cup

3	H	CHARLTON		W 3-2	3-1	Allen 6, 30, Dyson 39	Brown	Baker	Henry	Blanchflower	Norman	Mackay	Medwin	White	Smith R	Allen	Dyson
7/1			54,969	2:15		Leary 35, Lawrie 46	Duff	Sewell	Townsend	Hewie	Jago	Tocknell	Lawrie	Edwards	Leary	White	Summers
					Ref: J McLoughlin											

The script (written by most of the pundits) dictates that Charlton are going to get thrashed. The Valiants are reading a different version of it however: one that says they twice come back from two goals down to threaten an equaliser. The last goal is a spectacular leaping volley.

4	H	CREWE		W 5-1	3-1	Dyson 4, Smith 22, Mackay 32,	Brown	Baker	Henry	Blanchflower	Norman	Mackay	Jones	White	Smith R	Allen	Dyson
28/1			53,721	4:8		Tighe 27 [Jones 65, Allen 75]	Williamson	McGill	Campbell	Keery	Barnes	Shepherd	Stark	Tighe	Foster	Wheatley	Jones M
					Ref: R Leafe											

Crewe were annihilated 2-13 here last season and desperately wanted to play Spurs again to prove a point. Their wish is granted. They at least manage to keep the score respectable. Crewe had beaten Chelsea, but their only glory today comes when Tighe beats two to slot the ball home.

5	A	ASTON VILLA		W 2-0	2-0	Neal 18 (og), Jones 40	Brown	Baker	Henry	Blanchflower	Norman	Mackay	Jones	White	Smith R	Allen	Dyson
18/2			69,672	7			Sidebottom	Lynn	Neal	Crowe	Dugdale	Thomson	MacEwan	O'Neill	Hitchens	Wylie	McParland
					Ref: E Crawford											

Villa make a game of it for nearly 20 minutes, but then a stinging Jones drive is deflected into their net. Jones at least gets the credit for the second goal (a neat half-volley). A demoralised Villa side then get really rough. McParland is booked when he treads on Mackay's hand.

QF	A	SUNDERLAND		D 1-1	1-0	Jones 9	Brown	Baker	Henry	Blanchflower	Norman	Mackay	Jones	White	Smith R	Allen	Dyson
4/3			63,000	2:6		McPheat 50	Wakeham	Nelson	Ashurst	Anderson	Hurley	McNab	Hooper	Fagarty	Lawther	McPheat	Dillon
					Ref: A Murdoch											

Jones heads in a half-cleared corner to give Spurs an important early goal, but they fail to kill the game off. When McPheat equalises, the Roker Roar (and subsequent pitch invasion) threatens to inspire the Rokeries to a double-ending victory. Spurs' mighty defence stays solid.

QF	H	SUNDERLAND		W 5-0	3-0	Allen 28, Smith 32, Dyson 45, 54,	Brown	Baker	Henry	Blanchflower	Norman	Mackay	Jones	White	Smith R	Allen	Dyson
R	8/3		64,797	2:6		[Mackay 73]	Wakeham	Nelson	Ashurst	Harvey	Hurley	Anderson	Hooper	Fagarty	Lawther	McPheat	Dillon
					Ref: W Clements											

The gates at White Hart Lane are closed half an hour before kick-off. With no Roker Roar, Second Division Sunderland are soon cut down to size. Dillon and McPheat are both aged 18 and overall its own v boys as Spurs wrap up the tie up by the time the half-time whistle sounds.

SF	N	BURNLEY		W 3-0	1-0	Smith 31, 51, Jones 89	Brown	Baker	Henry	Blanchflower	Norman	Mackay	Jones	White	Smith R	Allen	Dyson
18/3			69,968	4			Blacklaw	Angus	Elder	Joyce	Adamson	Miller	Connelly	McIlroy	Pointer	Robson	Harris
	(At Villa Park)					Ref: K Collinge											

The Spurs defence weather a lot of pressure from Burnley, who dominate the first and last 30 minutes of the match. Smith eases the pressure by slamming home a loose ball for the first goal and then dispatching a half-clearance for number two. Spurs have won thrice here this season.

F	N	LEICESTER		W 2-0	0-0	Smith 69, Dyson 77	Brown	Baker	Henry	Blanchflower	Norman	Mackay	Jones	White	Smith R	Allen	Dyson
6/5			100,000	6			Banks	Chalmers	Norman	McLintock	King	Appleton	Riley	Walsh	McIlmoyle	Keyworth	Cheesebrough
	(At Wembley)					Ref: J Kelly											

An unusually quiet and jittery Spurs fail to trouble lively Leicester in the first period. The match turns when the Wembley injury jinx picks on Chalmers, who is a passenger following a knee injury. The tension ends with Smith slams in Dyson's cross. Dyson soon heads in the second.

158

	P	W	D	L	Home F	A	W	D	L	Away F	A	Pts	Odds & ends
1 TOTTENHAM	42	15	3	3	65	28	16	1	4	50	27	66	Double wins: (11) Arsenal, Aston Villa, Birmingham, Blackburn,
2 Sheffield Wed	42	15	4	2	45	17	8	8	5	33	30	58	Blackpool, Bolton, Chelsea, Everton, Nottingham F, Preston, West Ham.
3 Wolves	42	17	2	2	61	32	8	5	8	42	43	57	Double losses: (0).
4 Burnley	42	11	4	6	58	40	11	3	7	44	37	51	
5 Everton	42	13	4	4	47	23	9	2	10	40	46	50	Won from behind: (8) Bolton (a), Bolton (h), Newcastle (a), Cardiff (h),
6 Leicester	42	12	5	4	54	31	6	5	10	33	39	45	Blackburn (h), Arsenal (h), Chelsea (a), Sheffield W (h).
7 Manchester U	42	14	5	2	58	20	4	4	13	30	56	45	Lost from in front: (3) Burnley (a), Cardiff (a), Newcastle (h).
8 Blackburn	42	12	3	6	48	34	3	10	8	29	42	43	
9 Aston Villa	42	13	3	5	48	28	4	6	11	30	49	43	High spots: Scintillating start with eleven straight wins.
10 West Brom	42	10	3	8	43	32	8	2	11	24	39	41	Accomplishing the mighty double in breathtaking style.
11 Arsenal	42	12	3	6	44	35	3	8	10	33	50	41	Being arguably the greatest English club side ever.
12 Chelsea	42	10	5	6	61	48	5	2	14	37	52	37	Smashing records all over the place.
13 Manchester C	42	10	3	8	41	30	3	6	12	38	60	37	
14 Nott'm Forest	42	8	7	6	34	33	6	2	13	28	45	37	Low spots: Easing off at the end and failing to set a new points record.
15 Cardiff	42	11	5	5	34	26	2	6	13	26	59	37	Not entering the League Cup. Even with a semi-reserve side they could
16 West Ham	42	12	4	5	53	31	1	6	14	24	57	36	have done the treble (though they could also have blown the double).
17 Fulham	42	8	8	5	39	39	6	0	15	33	56	36	Attendances at home were often disappointingly low.
18 Bolton	42	9	5	7	38	29	3	6	12	20	44	35	
19 Birmingham	42	10	4	7	35	31	4	2	15	27	53	34	
20 Blackpool	42	9	3	9	44	34	3	6	12	24	39	33	
21 Newcastle	42	7	7	7	51	49	4	3	14	35	60	32	Ever-presents: (4) Allen, Blanchflower, Henry, White.
22 Preston	42	7	6	8	28	25	3	4	14	15	46	30	Hat-tricks: (2) Jones, Smith.
	924	245	97	120	1029	695	120	97	245	695	1029	924	Leading scorer: Smith (33).

	Appearances Lge	FAC	Goals Lge	FAC	Tot
Allen, Les	42	7	23	4	27
Baker, Peter	41	7	1		1
Barton, Ken	1				
Blanchflower, Danny	42	7	6		6
Brown, Bill	41	7			
Dyson, Terry	40	7	12	5	17
Henry, Ron	42	7			
Hollowbread, John	1				
Jones, Cliff	29	6	15	4	19
Mackay, Dave	37	7	4	2	6
Marchi, Tony	6				
Medwin, Terry	14	1	5		5
Norman, Maurice	41	7	4		4
Saul, Frank	6		3		3
Smith, John	1				
Smith, Robert	36	7	28	5	33
White, John	42	7	13		13
(own-goals)			1	1	2
17 players used	462	77	115	21	136

160   TOTTENHAM HOTSPUR: CHAMPIONS OF ENGLAND

THE MEN WHO MADE SOCCER HISTORY

Centre forward
Bobby Smith
43 games   33 goals

Left half
Dave Mackay
44 games   6 goals

Outside right
Cliff Jones
35 games   19 goals

Goalkeeper
Bill Brown
48 games

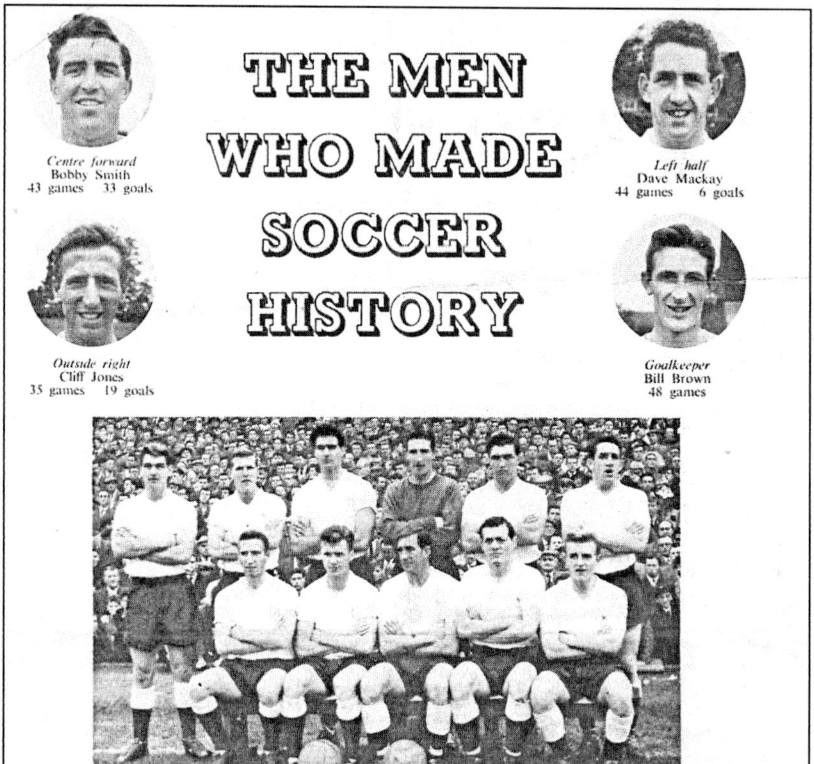

Super Spurs, winners of the Cup and League in 49 games. *Back:* Henry, Baker, Norman, Brown, Smith, Mackay. *Front:* Jones, White, Blanchflower, Allen, Dyson.

Right back
Peter Baker
48 games   1 goal

Manager
Billy Nicholson

Right half
Danny Blanchflower
49 games   6 goals

Centre half
Maurice Norman
48 games   4 goals

Inside right
John White
49 games   13 goals

Left back
Ron Henry
49 games

Inside left
Les Allen
49 games   27 goals

Outside left
Terry Dyson
47 games   17 goals

DESERT ISLAND BOOKS WOULD LIKE TO THANK THE FOLLOWING FOR THEIR CONTRIBUTION, AND FOR THEIR CHOICE OF THE MOST INVALUABLE TOTTENHAM HOTSPUR PLAYER:

Eric Church; Dave Franklin (Danny Blanchflower); Peter Glover (Dave Mackay);
Brian Judson; Gerald Kat, Nigel Kat; Bruce Lewis (Danny Blanchflower);
Elaine Lewis (Danny Blanchflower); Andy Porter (Danny Blanchflower);
Leon Ruskin (Ron Burgess); Paul Smith; Richard Stocken